KF
479
.Z9
J33
1997

Chicago Public Library

W9-BLH-554

ORIOLE

What are my rights? : 95 questions

What Are My Rights?

95 Questions and Answers
About Teens and the Law

By Thomas A. Jacobs, J.D.

free spirit
PUBLISHiNG

Works
for kids

CHICAGO PUBLIC LIBRARY
PARK BRANCH
N. OKETO   60656

DISCARD

Copyright © 1997 by Thomas A. Jacobs

All rights reserved under International and Pan-American Copyright Conventions. Unless otherwise noted, no part of this book may be reproduced, stored in a retrieval system, or transmitted in any form or by any means, electronic, mechanical, photocopying, recording or otherwise, without express written permission of the publisher, except for brief quotations or critical reviews.

Publisher's Note: The information contained in this book is not intended to supersede the advice of parents or legal counsel. Specific laws differ from one jurisdiction to another. Contact a local library, lawyer, or court to learn about the laws in your state or province.

At the time of this writing, all facts and figures cited are the most current available, and all Web site URLs are accurate and active. Please keep in mind that URLs change and sites come and go. When in doubt, use a search engine.

Library of Congress Cataloging-in-Publication Data

Jacobs, Thomas A.
    What are my rights? : 95 questions and answers about teens and the law / by Thomas A. Jacobs.
       p.   cm.
    Includes bibliographical references and index.
    Summary: Provides information to help the reader understand laws, recognize responsibilities, and appreciate rights especially in relation to parents, school, job, and personal matters.
    ISBN 1-57542-028-7
    1. Teenagers—Legal status, laws, etc.—United States—Juvenile literature. 2. Minors—United States—Juvenile works. 3. Children's rights—United States—Juvenile works. [1. Teenagers—Legal status, laws, etc. 2. Children's rights. 3. Law.]
    I. Title
KF479.Z9J33   1997
346.7301'35—dc21   97-8599
                                                                       CIP
                                                                      AC

Edited by Jay E. Johnson, Elizabeth Verdick, and Pamela Espeland
Cover design by Circus Design
Book interior design by chämeleon logic
Index prepared by Eileen Quam and Theresa Wolner

10 9 8 7 6 5 4 3
Printed in the United States of America

Free Spirit Publishing Inc.
400 First Avenue North, Suite 616
Minneapolis, MN 55401–1724
(612) 338-2068
help4kids@freespirit.com
www.freespirit.com

"The One Thing Teens Want Most from Life" chart on page 3 is reprinted by permission of the Horatio Alger Association for Distinguished Americans, Inc., in partnership with the National Association of Secondary School Principals.

The quotation by NBA All-Star A.C. Green on page 69 is from "Victory," reprinted by permission of the A.C. Green Youth Foundation, P.O. Box 1709, Phoenix, Arizona 85001; 1-800-AC YOUTH (1-800-229-6884).

The SADD "Contract for Life" on page 115 is reprinted by permission of Bill Cullinane, National Director of SADD.

The quiz about sexual harassment on page 124 is from *Sexual Harassment and Teens* by Susan Strauss with Pamela Espeland (Minneapolis: Free Spirit Publishing Inc., 1992). Used with permission of the publisher.

Dedication

This book is dedicated to my five children, who were a continuing inspiration throughout their teen years. Their mother and I survived their adolescence, as most parents do.

Also to my family's next generation of teens: Kylie, Alexandra, Cody, Netaya, Shasheena, Pauly, Aaron, Kali, Taylor, and Austin.

Acknowledgments

You would not be reading this book were it not for the following persons. Heartfelt thanks and appreciation are extended to Michelle Colla, Pamela Davis, Ken Reeves, Jami Taylor, Sue Tone, and Kathy Welch. The reference librarians at the Phoenix Public Library, Scottsdale City Library, Arizona State University College of Law Library, and State of Arizona Law Library are dedicated public servants who saved me untold hours of research time.

Thanks also to a special group of Girl Scouts—Troop 399, who reviewed and commented on the original work. This includes Troop Leader Maria del Mar Verdin, assistant Caroline Como, and scouts Andrea Arenas, Amanda Bernardo, Nicole Croci, Kristin Reynolds, Vanessa Schafer, Amanda and Jessica Scharlau, Jamie Stewart, and Scout mom Kristen Scharlau.

Editor Jay E. Johnson put me through the worst month of my life—resulting in a book vastly improved in quality and content from its earlier, self-published edition. Thanks, Jay.

Waiting six years for the right publisher has its rewards. Free Spirit publisher Judy Galbraith, editors Elizabeth Verdick and Pamela Espeland, and their support staff share in this effort. Thanks for your wisdom and assistance throughout this project.

Contents

R017054 7497
CHICAGO PUBLIC LIBRARY
ORIOLE PARK BRANCH
5201 N. OKETO   60656

Introduction

It was 2:00 in the morning. Fourteen-year-old Natalie's parents had gone to bed hours ago, and the house was quiet. Startled awake by the telephone, Natalie's mother listened as a police officer asked her to pick up her daughter at a friend's house.

Earlier that day, Natalie had gotten her parents' permission to spend the night at Christy's house. But Natalie hadn't mentioned that Christy's parents were out of town for the weekend. Word spread quickly, and it wasn't long before a loud and crowded party was underway.

After several calls from irate neighbors, the police came and broke up the party. Charges filed against the party-goers ranged from curfew violation to possession and consumption of alcohol, disturbing the peace, property damage, and resisting arrest. Natalie, like some of the other teenagers, was given a ticket for possession of beer.

Maybe you or a friend have been in a similar situation. Or maybe this hasn't happened to you. But if it did, would you know what to do if the police told you that you had broken the law?

- In 1990, there were 27 million juveniles ages 10–17 in the U.S.
- By the year 2010, there should be 33.8 million.

Source: *Juvenile Offenders and Victims: A National Report.* National Center for Juvenile Justice, 1995.

Situations like Natalie's happen all the time. Most of the teenagers at the party knew they were doing things their parents probably wouldn't approve of. But many had never really thought about the fact that they were also breaking several laws. It had never crossed their minds that their actions could lead to fines or an arrest. They were simply having a good time with friends.

Knowing about laws that affect you and others your age can help you make better decisions about what you should and shouldn't do. Being informed could help you to decide whether or not to:

- cut class
- use a fake ID
- obey your teacher
- smoke cigarettes
- make a crank call
- gamble
- get a job
- stay out really late
- get into a fight.

What Are My Rights? won't tell you everything you need to know about how laws are passed and enforced, and it won't tell you how the government works. It *will* tell you which laws affect you and why. It will also tell you what happens if you break the law and get caught. It will help you to understand the laws, recognize your responsibilities, and appreciate your rights. Each chapter has an introduction that orients you to certain issues, followed by question-and-answer sections that cover topics that concern you and your friends.

It wasn't too long ago that young people had no recognizable rights. During the last century, and as recently as thirty years ago, children were mainly considered the property of their parents. Many children and teenagers labored for twelve-hour days in horrible working conditions because they had no protection under the law. Thankfully, times have changed. You and other young people now have rights that protect you within your family, at school, on the job, at the doctor, and in your community.

Your state legislature and city council are responsible for seeing that laws exist to protect and serve youth and the community as a whole. The authority to act for the people in passing laws and enforcing them in the nation's courts comes from the United

The One Thing Teens Want Most from Life

Choices	All (%)	Boys (%)	Girls (%)
Happiness	28	23	32
Long/enjoyable life	16	18	14
Marriage/family	9	8	11
Financial success	8	11	5
Career success	8	9	6
Religious satisfaction	8	7	7
Love	7	6	7
Personal success	6	6	5
Personal contribution to society	2	3	2
Friends	2	3	1
Health	2	2	2
Education	2	1	2

Source: *The Mood of American Youth* survey taken in April, 1996, by the Horatio Alger Association. 1,500 teens were surveyed; 938 responded. Because some teens didn't respond, the figures don't total 100%.

States Constitution, the Bill of Rights,* and state constitutions (which closely follow the U.S. Constitution). Just as federal and state laws in America regarding teenagers differ, the laws of Canada vary among the provinces. Some Canadian laws and related community resources are included in this book, along with U.S. laws and resources.

Many teenagers have questions about the law—"What if my best friend is shoplifting?" "Is it illegal to be in a gang?" "Could I go to jail?" "What if my parents die?" "What if I win the lottery?"—but they don't know where to turn for answers. *What Are My Rights?* is designed to be your first stop for exploring these and other legal questions. It covers childhood issues as well as concerns of the later teen years. The first chapters address parental authority, your rights at school, and issues of law while you're on the job. Other chapters discuss rights of a more personal nature, those that

---

* See Chapter 2, pages 30–31.

deal with your body and growing up. The final chapter considers the more somber side of the law—the consequences of willful misconduct or bad judgment—and offers basic information about the legal system.

Throughout this book, you'll find "FYI" (For Your Information) sections with descriptions of resources—including other books, national organizations, and Web sites—that you can turn to for information and advice.* You'll also find listings for toll-free telephone numbers and hotlines. But if something in this book applies to you, it's best to speak *first* with someone you know and trust. If possible, talk things over with your parents. Consider telling a teacher, school counselor, or youth leader at your place of worship. Think of another adult you can talk to—someone who will listen, understand, and give you good advice. You probably know at least one adult who will help you and stand by you.

In this book, you'll also find true stories of teenagers who have spoken out or changed the law to benefit youth. You'll read about different ways you can stand up for yourself and invoke your rights. Knowledge is power. As you learn more about legal issues, think about what *you* might do to bring about positive change at home, at work, at school, and in your community.

---

* If you don't have access to the Internet at home or at school, ask at your local library about free community Internet access.

Chapter 1

You and Your Family

*"At our best level of existence, we are parts of a family,
and at our highest level of achievement,
we work to keep the family alive."*

Maya Angelou, American writer, activist, and actress

Did you know that 189 countries, including the United States and Canada, have signed a Declaration of the Rights of the Child? The Declaration was passed by the United Nations in 1989, and it calls for all countries to guarantee that you have:

- a childhood without adult responsibilities
- a happy family life
- a school that educates you according to your learning needs and interests
- a doctor who knows your name
- a safe neighborhood
- a chance to achieve and succeed in life.

A teenagers' bill of rights might also include the right to be heard and listened to by others, the right to receive good guidance, and the right to receive fair treatment and reasonable discipline from authority figures.

"The rights to conceive and raise one's children have been deemed essential . . . basic civil rights of man . . . and rights far more precious . . . than property rights."—U.S. Supreme Court (1972), *Stanley v. Illinois*

Because these rights aren't guaranteed to all young people, the process of safeguarding yourself and your future starts at home. In fact, many of the rules that you have to follow at home are actually rooted in the law. While some of these rules may seem too strict or unfair, they're designed to protect you. Understanding your rights and responsibilities at home can bring you closer to reaching your goals in life.

"What does adoption mean?"

Under special circumstances, you may receive a new parent or parents. If your parents die, for example, or agree to let someone else raise you, the court may allow that person to adopt you. Most of the time, young children or babies are adopted, but in certain situations adults and teenagers may also be adopted. This often occurs in cases where there's a long-term relationship between a stepparent and other family members.

Over 100,000 adoptions take place in the United States each year. These include children born in the U.S., as well as children brought into the U.S. from other countries. In most states, you must be eighteen to adopt a child. Some states require the adult to be ten years older than the child who is being adopted. Other states have no age restrictions. You don't necessarily have to be married to adopt a child. Single people—straight, gay, and lesbian—have become adoptive parents of children of all ages.

"Courts are not free to take children from parents simply by deciding another home appears more advantageous." —U.S. Supreme Court (1993), *DeBoer v. DeBoer*

If your parents are divorced and your mother or father remarries, your new stepparent may adopt you if your other parent agrees. This is called a *stepparent adoption,* and it must also be approved by a judge. If you're over a certain age, usually ten or twelve years old, you must appear at the hearing and agree with the adoption. The judge will ask you if you want your stepfather or stepmother to be your legal parent, and if you want your last name to be changed.

During the adoption process, you may meet with a social worker and a lawyer. They, in turn, meet with your prospective new parents and gather information to help the judge decide if the adoption will be allowed. A complete investigation is done, and recommendations are made to the court. The investigation, called an *adoptive home study,* considers the motivation to adopt, finances, criminal history, family background, education, work history, and references from relatives and nonrelatives. If the court has any concerns, the adoption may be delayed. The bottom line in any adoption is whether it's best for the child. While most adoptions are granted, occasionally the judge may decide that it's not in the child's best interests.

> Once legally free for adoption, children wait an average of ten months before being adopted.
>
> **Source:** *Child Abuse and Neglect: A Look at the States: CWLA Stat Book 1995,* Child Welfare League of America

If you were adopted when you were a baby, what are you entitled to know about the adoption and its circumstances? Privacy for birth parents, adoptive parents, and adopted children is still the general rule. Each state has its own laws regarding the disclosure of records. Depending on where you live, you may be able to find out *nonidentifying* information—information that tells you about your biological parents without revealing their names. Or, in some situations, once you're an adult, you may be able to find out *identifying* information—including their names.

You may also be able to learn about your birth parents' medical history. Contact the court where the adoption took place and ask for this information.

For a state-by-state chart showing how old you must be for adoption records to be made available to you, see pages 175–177.

The Adoption Directory, 2d ed., by Ellen Paul (Gale Research, Inc., 1995). Information about adoption search agencies, support groups, and advocacy programs.

Where Are My Birth Parents? A Guide for Teenage Adoptees by Karen Gravelle and Susan Fischer (Walker and Company, 1993). How and why adopted children may try to locate and get to know their birth parents; possible psychological benefits and problems associated with that process.

Adopt: Assistance, Information, Support
http://www.adopting.org/ar.html
A gateway site to vast amounts of information for and about adoptive parents, children, and teens.

Immigration and Naturalization Service (INS)
For information on international adoptions and the rules and regulations of the INS, contact your state service office or regional center:

- Central Region, P.O. Box 152122, Irving, TX 75015-2122; (214) 767-7769
- Eastern Region, 75 Lower Weldon Street, St. Albans, VT 05479-0001; (802) 527-3160
- Western Region, 24000 Avila Road, 2d Floor, Laguna Niguel, CA 92656; (714) 643-4880

The National Adoption Center
1-800-862-3678
http://www.adopt.org/adopt
Information and referrals related to conducting an adoption search, putting a child up for adoption, and much more.

"What is foster care? How long does it last?"

Half a million children live in foster homes, group homes, emergency receiving homes, or child-crisis centers across the U.S. Twenty-four percent of these children spend between one to two years in out-of-home care.

There are many reasons why young people are moved to out-of-home care, including neglect, abandonment, or child abuse.* If the state learns that a child is being maltreated in some way, the child may be removed. It's the state's responsibility to protect its children. If removed, a child is either placed with relatives, friends, or—as a last resort—into a foster home.

The people who operate foster homes are licensed, trained, and monitored by a state agency—usually Child Protective Services (CPS). If you're placed in foster care, you'll receive medical, dental, psychological, and educational services. An attorney or guardian may be appointed to look out for you and to discuss your situation and represent you in court. Depending on your age, you may have the opportunity to appear in court with your lawyer. The judge may want to hear from you about your situation.

- In 1994, over 215,000 young people ages 12–17 in the U.S. were reported as victims of child abuse or neglect.
- Approximately 21% of teenagers ages 13–17 were involved in verified reports of abuse and neglect in 1993.
- Neglect accounts for almost 50% of maltreatment reports, followed by physical abuse (22%), sexual abuse (13%), emotional maltreatment (5%), and medical neglect (2%).
- Child abuse reports increase an average of 4% each year—49% since 1986.

Sources: *Child Maltreatment 1994: Reports from the States to the National Center on Child Abuse and Neglect*, U.S. Department of Health and Human Services (1996); *Child Abuse and Neglect: A Look at the States: CWLA Stat Book 1995*, Child Welfare League of America

The goal of every court and agency responsible for your care is to work toward finding you a permanent home. This may mean returning you to your parents when they're ready to provide safe care, or finding you an adoptive home. A lot depends on why you were originally placed in foster care. If the problems have been solved and you can be safely returned to your parents, the court may allow it. Otherwise, after you've spent six to twelve months in foster care, other plans will be considered.

State laws regarding your rights and your parents' rights have changed in the past few years. Parents are required to show by their actions, not words, that they intend to work toward your

---

* See Chapter 4, pages 74–76, for more information on abuse and neglect.

return. They must resolve whatever problem caused you to be placed in foster care—by, for example, getting counseling, going into drug rehabilitation, or taking parenting classes. If too much time passes without any positive results, alternative plans must be made. Although there's no time limit on a foster home placement, state and federal laws discuss a "permanent" home for all children. This may mean a return to your parents, placement with relatives or friends, or adoption. Each case is considered on an individual basis by the courts and social workers.

You don't lose any rights while you're in foster care. The agency responsible for you must see that all of your needs are met and that you're in a safe environment. You should receive medical and dental care, as well as schooling and recreation. In foster care, you have to follow house rules regarding hygiene, curfew, and study and recreation time.

Once you turn eighteen and become an adult, foster care may end. Some states allow you to remain in foster care if you're still in high school or if special circumstances exist. If you still need care after you're eighteen, Adult Protective Services (APS) will provide it.

Coping as a Foster Child by Geraldine M. Blomquist and Paul Blomquist (Rosen Publishing Group, 1991). Information for teens facing foster care. Covers therapeutic foster homes, adoption, independent living programs, and care for unwed mothers and their babies.

"What happens to me if my parents get a divorce?"

If your parents get a divorce, it doesn't mean that they're no longer your parents, or that they no longer love you. Children are not the cause of their parents' divorce—and they have no reason to feel guilty or blame themselves. If your parents have divorced and you feel guilty about it, get help so you can work things out in your life. Contact a school counselor, who may recommend that you talk to a trained professional. Or let your mother or father know that the divorce is bothering you, and you need help dealing with it.

Can your parents force you to go to counseling if you're troubled by divorce (or any other issue)? Yes. They can arrange for the whole family to attend counseling, or individual counseling for one or two of you. Since you have little choice but to go, keep an open mind. It may seem awkward at first, but you'll soon find yourself opening up and feeling better. Relationship issues don't happen overnight, and healing also takes time. Talk with your friends and you'll see that you're not alone in your thoughts, fears, and concerns.

If your parents get a divorce, decisions have to be made that directly affect you. You may have questions: "Do I have to move?" "Will I be separated from my brothers and sisters?" "Will I get to see the parent I don't live with?" A court may help your parents with these decisions and, depending on your age, you may be asked for your opinion on what *you* want to happen.

A lawyer may be appointed to represent you if your parents don't agree on visitation issues or where you should live. Tell your lawyer *exactly* what you feel about these issues and why. This is the *only* way to be sure your wishes will be considered by the judge before a decision is made.

Although the ultimate question in each divorce case is "What is in the child's best interests?" the states don't follow the same laws in determining the answer. Some states give preference to the desires of the child; others don't. Some appoint lawyers or guardians to speak for the children; others don't. In most cases, though, the results are the same, since "best interests" is the goal in all jurisdictions. Both parents are considered in custody disputes— those that concern which parent you'll live with. In the past, the law tended to support automatic custody with the mother, but today fathers are often given custody of their children.

Courts grant either sole custody to one parent, or joint or shared custody to both parents. In a *sole custody* situation, you'll live with one of your parents and visit the other (for example, on weekends, holidays, and during the summer). If your noncustodial parent lives out of state, you may spend all or part of the summer with that parent. The same is true for your brothers and sisters. Courts try to keep the children in a family together. If siblings are split up, arrangements may be made for frequent contact and visits.

Joint or *shared custody* requires both parents to agree on the living arrangements of the children. It allows both parents to share legal and physical custody of you and your brothers and sisters, with an even split of time and responsibilities throughout the year. You may live with your mother during the school year, and with your father during the summer and holidays. Or, if your parents live close by, especially in the same school district, you may alternate weeks or months at each parent's home.

The rule in custody situations should be whatever works out best for all of you. Be sure to speak up and let your parents know how you feel about the arrangements. Whatever is decided, give it a try for a period of time. If you feel strongly one way or the other, tell your parents. It's best to get your feelings out in the open. Speaking up may help change things. You'll also be helping your siblings if they feel the same way but are afraid to say anything.

If you find yourself unable to talk to anyone about divorce and custody worries, pay a visit to your school or public library. You'll find books and pamphlets written especially for children and teens that will help to answer some of your questions and concerns. Check one out—and maybe confide in a friend.

For a state-by-state chart about custody factors, see pages 178–179.

Coping in a Single Parent Home by Bill Wagonseller, Lynne C. Ruegamer, and Marie C. Harrington (Rosen Publishing Group, 1997). Covers survival skills, parental dating, searching for birth parents, tracking an absent parent, grief, support groups, and more.

Everything You Need to Know About Your Parents' Divorce by Linda Carlson Johnson (Rosen Publishing Group, 1994). Clear and basic information about what happens when parents divorce.

My Parents Are Getting Divorced: A Handbook for Kids. American Bar Association *Family Advocate,* Spring 1996 (Vol. 18, No. 4). Ask at your library or call toll-free 1-800-285-2221 to order a copy of this great little book.

When Divorce Hits Home: Keeping Yourself Together When Your Family Comes Apart by Thea Joselow and Beth Baruch Joselow (Avon Books, 1996). Written by a mother-daughter team, based on interviews with lots of kids who have been through the divorce of their parents.

"What is kidnapping?"

Kidnapping is defined as knowingly restraining someone with a specific intent to do something. This may be to collect a ransom, use a person as a hostage, or have someone do involuntary work. Other intentions may be to injure a person or to interfere with the operation of an airplane, bus, train, or other form of transportation. Kidnapping may be a felony, depending on the circumstances. If someone is convicted of kidnapping, it's not uncommon for that person to receive a jail or prison sentence.

Custodial interference, sometimes called *parental kidnapping,* happens when one parent keeps a child from the other parent who has legal custody. Statistics indicate that over 350,000 children are kidnapped

If you're a victim of kidnapping or custodial interference, or if your brother or sister is in danger of being kidnapped, *take immediate action.* Call the police, dial 0 for an operator, or dial 911 for emergency assistance.

by family members every year. Specific state and federal laws against parental kidnapping carry stiff sentences for violation.

For example, say the court has placed you in the legal custody of your mother. Your father lives out of state and has holiday visits. After you spend two weeks with your father at Christmas, he decides not to return you to your mother. This is custodial interference and may be prosecuted as a crime.

If your parents agree that you can live with your father, however, they should ask the court to modify the custody order. Courts grant modification requests all the time. The key issue is what's best for you. If there's no risk of abuse or neglect, and the change is to your benefit, it will most likely be approved.

Let your opinion be heard in custody modification situations. Many courts want to know whether you agree with the change of custody. Feel free to write the court a letter. Or you may have the opportunity to go to court and speak with the judge. This is your chance to state your true feelings. If you're hesitant to speak up in your parents' presence, ask to talk to the judge alone. Many judges will allow this. You may be taken to the judge's office with your lawyer or guardian, where you can speak freely. The judge will see that your statements remain confidential.

The point is that *you* are the most important person in the case. Your opinion matters and should be heard. The results may not be 100 percent to your satisfaction, but speaking up gives you the chance to share your views and to make sure your concerns are taken into account.

"If my parents get a divorce, will I still get to visit my grandparents?"

Visitation is a big issue that gets decided in every divorce case. It starts with your parents. If your mother is given sole custody, your father will be granted visitation rights. Likewise, if your father is given sole custody, your mother will be granted visitation. This means the noncustodial parent will be able to see you on a regular basis, with set times and days. Or it may be more flexible, depending on what your parents agree on. The court will review the terms and, based on what's in your best interests, approve or modify them.

Over the past few years, grandparents have become active in asserting their requests for visits with grandchildren whose parents divorce. Many states have passed laws allowing grandparents to seek a court order for visits if they've been denied visitation by the parents. Some states require that a minimum period of time pass (three to six months) before the visits begin—a period where everyone can cool off after the divorce. Other courts require a hearing with an opportunity to oppose grandparent visits if a good reason exists. If visits are granted, the court will usually set forth a schedule that all are required to follow. Each case is unique; there's no specific formula that's followed with identical results each time.

> A new trend in litigation is the pursuit of visitation rights by grandparents following a stepparent adoption. Most states don't yet have specific laws on this subject, but the courts look to what's best for the child or teen being adopted. The traditional view was expressed by an Arizona court: "While we recognize that a grandparent's love, acceptance, and care may complement the role of parents . . . there is no legal right to visitation" following an adoption. (*In the Matter of Maricopa County Action No. JA-502394*, 1996)

Stepparents may also seek visitation rights. For example, if your mother and stepfather get a divorce, does your former stepfather have any visitation rights? Can you continue to visit the stepparent who's now legally out of the picture? State legislatures are now considering laws addressing parents who find themselves in this situation. Most states, at this time, don't provide stepparents with visitation rights. Some courts, however, will look at the whole picture, including how long the stepparent has been involved in your life, your opinion about visitation, and any other relevant factors. Courts have granted former stepparents visitation with their stepchildren. Again, the bottom line is what's best for you.

"Do my parents have to support me after they get divorced?"

Child support is a hot issue. Headlines scream "Deadbeat Dad Jailed," and names of nonpaying parents are displayed on billboards and wanted posters. Law enforcement officials plan sting operations and holiday arrests.

What's it all about? Why are fathers going to jail? What if mothers miss a support payment?

First, *all* parents have a legal duty and obligation to support their children. This includes divorced parents and those who never married. The *duty* to support a child means providing financial assistance to the custodial parent for the basic necessities of life— food, shelter, clothing, medical expenses, and education. The *obligation* may apply to either parent—mother or father. The court looks at the whole family situation, including both parents' earnings, standards of living, and debts, and the ages and needs of the children. Guidelines exist to help the court arrive at a fair child support figure. Once the amount is determined, the court makes an order and payments are scheduled to begin, usually on a monthly basis.

As children get older, support payments may be increased as the children's needs change and the cost of living rises. If a parent misses a payment or is occasionally late in paying, any dispute will probably be resolved without going back to court. However, if *no* payments are made, this becomes a serious matter. There's now a nationwide crackdown on parents who are behind in their payments. Why? Because taxpayers are paying millions of dollars to families on welfare who aren't being supported by responsible parents.

States are trying various methods to get parents to pay their child support. Some states are going public with billboards and wanted posters in an effort to embarrass "deadbeat" parents into paying. In Arizona, a parent who falls one month behind in child support payments can have his or her professional license (medical, law, therapist, etc.) or work permit/certificate suspended.

If your parents are divorced, their duty to support you continues until you turn eighteen or are emancipated.* Some states require child support to continue after your eighteenth birthday if you're still in high school. Once you graduate or get your Graduate Equivalency Diploma (GED), the legal obligation to support you ends. A number of states extend the support obligation beyond eighteen if you're physically or mentally disabled. Your parents may agree at the time of the divorce to cover your college or technical school expenses. This will obviously extend support past your eighteenth birthday, and such an agreement has been determined by the courts to be valid and enforceable.

Even if you're a teenage parent, you still have a duty and obligation to support your child(ren). Some states require the parents of a teenage mother or father to assist in the baby's support, but the birth parent, regardless of age, carries the primary responsibility.

"Can I 'divorce' my parents?"

In 1992, a Florida boy named Gregory K. got a court order terminating his mother's parental rights and giving him the legal right to become part of a new family. His birth father didn't contest the adoption. In effect, Gregory "divorced" his parents.

This was a unique case because it was filed by a child with help from his lawyer. Usually, the state or a child welfare agency files this type of lawsuit on behalf of a child. However, when Gregory was eleven, he decided he wanted to remain in the foster home where he'd lived for nine months. Because he'd been neglected and abused by his parents, Gregory had been in foster care for two years. He hadn't seen his mother in eighteen months. He thought she had forgotten about him. His new foster parents wanted to adopt him, and the court determined that this was best for Gregory.

---

* To learn about emancipation, see Chapter 5, pages 96–98.

Gregory's case opened the door for a whole new discussion and review of children's rights. State legislatures and courts across the country are paying attention to the reasonable and legitimate demands of minors. The emphasis now is on "permanency" for all children and teenagers in foster care. If kids are unable to return home or be placed with relatives, alternative permanent homes are sought. Public and private agencies are taking legal action toward terminating parents' rights in the appropriate cases.

This doesn't mean that because you don't like being grounded, you can go to court and get new parents. This is a serious decision that's limited in its application. Only in the most extreme situation, and usually as a last resort, will the legal rights of a parent be terminated.

If things are seriously wrong in your family and you have questions or problems that you've been keeping to yourself, find someone you trust and can talk to. A school counselor, teacher, clergy member, or adult friend or family member may be someone you can turn to. Don't let the situation get so out of control that your health and safety are at risk. Community groups or Child Protective Services (CPS) are good resources for assistance.

"Who has the right to discipline me?"

"You can't tell me what to do." "I don't have to—you're not my parent!" "If you touch me, I'll call the police!" In the heat of an argument, you may say things like this to a parent, stepparent, guardian, or teacher. Who has the right to discipline you?

The law gives your parents control over your life until you become an adult. In fact, the U.S. Supreme Court has stated that the custody, care, and nurturance of a child belong first to the parents, and that it's their duty to prepare you for independence.* This means that your parents can decide:

---

* Exceptions to parental control are discussed in Chapter 5, pages 95–117.

- what school you'll go to
- when you'll be able to drive
- what religion (if any) to raise you in
- when you can get a job
- if you can marry before you're eighteen.

Your parents or guardians, however, are *not* free to discipline you beyond reason. Every state has child protection laws and an agency to investigate abused, neglected, and abandoned children. If Child Protective Services (CPS) determines that the discipline or punishment you receive is excessive or harmful, whether physically, sexually, or emotionally, they may remove you from your home to a safer environment.

Strict "rules of the house," or what you may consider harsh punishment, isn't sufficient for CPS or the police to get involved. The government may not interfere with the duties of a parent to raise a child unless abuse has occurred or the threat of abuse or neglect exists.

Abuse and neglect are specifically defined by state law.* *Abuse* may include physical, sexual, and emotional harm. *Neglect* may mean physical, emotional, or educational deprivation. Emotional neglect by a parent isn't easy to pin down or prove. Not all states recognize emotional harm to a child or teenager as requiring action or intervention. Typical symptoms of emotional harm include poor performance at school, depression, and antisocial or destructive behavior.

In a 1992 case, a ten-year-old child in Iowa was removed from her mother's home. Following her parents' divorce, she became depressed and developed an eating disorder. Her mother provoked the child's adverse feelings against her father and encouraged her to eat in order to cope with her stress. At one point, the 5'3" girl weighed 290 pounds. The court considered this a form of emotional abuse and placed her in a residential treatment program.

---

* See Chapter 4, pages 74–76, for more information on abuse and neglect.

Although emotional neglect is difficult to define, a California court stated in 1993 that "persons of common intelligence would not have to guess whether someone was maltreating their child to the point of causing severe emotional harm."

The bottom line, however, is that you're required to follow the rules set by your parents. If there's a disagreement about driving or your curfew, for example, talk about it with your parents. Ask them to sit down with you and calmly discuss the situation. Maybe you can reach a compromise. If not, you'll still feel better for getting your feelings out in the open.

Try these ideas for talking with your parents:

- Pick a quiet time.
- Keep distractions to a minimum—no TV or radio.
- Don't start talks when your friends are over.
- Stay calm and don't swear.
- State your side and why.
- Ask your parents to state their position—and listen to what they say.

While you're at school, teachers and other school staff take the place of your parents. Misconduct will result in some form of disciplinary action—detention time, extra assignments, or lost privileges. In extreme cases, suspension or expulsion may occur. School policy may also permit paddling or spanking, which the U.S. Supreme Court has determined is not cruel and unusual punishment under the Eighth Amendment. School districts vary in the use of corporal punishment to discipline students.*

Bringing Up Parents: The Teenager's Handbook by Alex J. Packer, Ph.D. (Free Spirit Publishing, 1992). Straight talk and specific suggestions for getting along with parents, having fewer fights, and gaining more respect and freedom.

---

* See Chapter 2, pages 37–38.

"Can my parents force me to follow their religion?"

The First Amendment to the U.S. Constitution guarantees all Americans freedom of religion. This isn't limited to adults. Children and teenagers enjoy the same right, which is balanced with the fundamental rights of parents to raise their children without government interference.

What this means for you is that the government and the courts won't get involved if you and your parents disagree about religious beliefs or practices. As long as you're safe and your basic needs are provided for (food, shelter, clothing, and medical care), the state can't interfere with your family. Your parents are free to decide what church to attend, how often, and what practices will be honored in the home.

If you're at risk of being abused or neglected because of your parents' religious beliefs, the police or Child Protective Services (CPS) may step in to ensure your safety. For example, if you were in need of a blood transfusion or other urgent medical care, and your parents refused to give their consent due to their religious beliefs, the court could get involved. In a life-threatening situation, or one where there's a risk of permanent disability, the court has the right to order the appropriate medical care for you.

Occasionally, a hospital or doctor will contact the court to assist with difficult emergency cases. In 1994, the U.S. Supreme Court stated that parents may be free to become martyrs themselves, but they are not free to make martyrs of their children (*Prince v. Massachusetts,* 1994). In following that decision, a Minnesota court stated that "although one is free to believe what one will, religious freedom ends when one's conduct offends the law by, for example, endangering a child's life" (*Lundman v. McKown,* 1995).

In the Minnesota case, an eleven-year-old boy was diagnosed with juvenile-onset diabetes. His parents were Christian Scientists, a religion that believes in prayer as the proper treatment for illness. The boy died because he was denied medical treatment. In discussing the difference between the freedom to believe and the freedom to act, the court upheld the government's right to restrict acts based on religious beliefs. In other words, people can't claim religion as a reason for not paying taxes, violating child labor laws, marrying more than one person at a time, or refusing medical care for their children.

As you get older and think about the role of religion in your life, talk with your parents. Share your ideas and feelings. Talk with your friends who may belong to different faiths. What is their relationship with their parents on the subject of religion? It won't be long before you're independent and able to worship as you choose.

"Can my parents keep me from watching certain TV shows?"

There's an ongoing debate about the effect of media violence on young people. Numerous studies indicate a strong relationship between media exposure and the increasingly aggressive behavior and attitude of some teens. Young children in particular are highly impressionable and often fail to distinguish between fantasy and reality.

Of special concern is the violence shown on television. What used to be considered the "family hour" (6:00 to 8:00 P.M.), or children's TV-viewing time before school and early weekend mornings, now often has programs with violent or mature themes. Research supports the conclusion that TV violence, including cartoon violence, causes children to be less sensitive to pain and suffering. It makes them more fearful of the world in general, and it may cause some children to become more aggressive.

The Children's Television Act of 1990 limited commercials during children's programming. In 1996, Congress passed the Telecommunications Act. This federal law requires televisions made from 1998 on to come equipped with a special computer chip (called a "violence chip" or "V-chip") that allows parents to block certain shows. The television industry agreed to establish a ratings system that would serve as a guide for parents and trigger the V-chip. If your parents don't want you to see particular shows or watch TV at certain times, they can activate the V-chip, preventing your TV from showing the scheduled programs.

> • The average American child watches 25 hours of television each week—some as much as 11 hours a day.
> • A typical 11-year-old has seen 100,000 acts of violence on TV, including 8,000 murders.
> • A 1995 *USA Today* survey of readers indicated that 90% support the V-chip.
>
> **Sources:** Legislative history of the Telecommunications Act of 1996, found in *U.S. Code Congressional and Administrative News*, 104th Congress, Vol. 1, pp. 116–117

"What is a will? Can I write one for myself?"

Because of your age and active life, the idea of a will or inheritance may be the last thing on your mind. There's always the possibility, however, that you may be on the receiving end of a will (as a beneficiary). You may also own property that you would like to leave to someone if you die.

A will, or last will and testament, is a written statement indicating what will happen to your property after you die. (See page 25 for an example of a basic form.) You have to be eighteen to write a will, but it's something to think about before your eighteenth birthday. Property includes anything you own: clothes, games, books, savings bonds, money, or a car. If it's legally yours, you have the right to give it away.

> If your mother or father is a state senator in the state of **New York,** they may leave their senate seat to you in their will—not the *office* itself, but the *chair* they used while in office. Otherwise, you may buy it for $25.

There are two ways your property passes to someone else:

• If you have a will when you die, then you're *testate,* which means the directions stated in your will must be followed. You can leave your property to anyone or any organization or cause—it's entirely your decision. As long as your directions are legal and not against public policy, the law requires that your wishes must be carried out.

- If you die without a will, you're *intestate*, meaning the inheritance laws of your state apply. These laws spell out where your property goes—usually to family members. As a last resort, when there are no family or extended family members (brothers, sisters, aunts, uncles, or cousins), the property goes to the state.

You don't have to hire a lawyer to prepare your will. You may write it yourself in your own handwriting (a *holographic* will), or you can buy a standard form for a will at a stationery store. If you have a lot of money or property, it's advisable to speak with a lawyer about your wishes, but it's not required.

You may have heard the word *probate*. This is the legal process, through the court, of handling a person's property after death. Probate courts are responsible for supervising the distribution of the property, paying the debts that exist, and seeing that the interests of the people, organizations, and causes named in the will (if there is a will) are protected. It's not always necessary to involve the court; each case is unique. Check the laws in your state.

"What if my parents die without a will?"

If your parents die with a will (testate), their property goes to those persons, organizations, or causes named in the will. The law doesn't require that parents leave everything—or even anything—to their children. Property may be left as the testator chooses. The only way the will may be ignored and not followed is if it can be proved that the person was mentally incompetent at the time of writing the will. In other words, if you can prove that Uncle Austin was crazy when he wrote his will and left a fortune to his favorite Italian restaurant, the will may be set aside. This is called a *will contest.*

Last Will and Testament
of

_____

I, _____ of _____
          (Name)   (Address)

declare this to be my Last Will and Testament.

ONE: I cancel all Wills that I have made before this Will.

TWO: All property owned by me at my death is hereby given to _____

(Specify the gifts and persons who are to receive them.)

_____

_____.

THREE: If _____ dies before me, I give all the property which I own at my death to_____.

FOUR: If after my death it is necessary that a guardian be appointed for any child of mine, I appoint _____.

LAST WILL AND TESTAMENT OF

_____
          (Your signature)

_____
          (Date)

This Will was signed by its maker on the date written above in the presence of those signed below as witnesses.

_____   _____
          (Name)   (Address)

_____   _____
          (Name)   (Address)

NOTE: This is an example of a basic will—it's not an official form. States differ regarding the specifics. Consult your local court and/or a lawyer.

If your parents die without a will (intestate), their property follows the laws of the state where they lived. Typical intestate laws provide for the property to be split among surviving family members. Immediate family comes first, and depending on who's available, the right to inherit branches out to extended family members. If there are no surviving family members, the property goes to the state.

You're not excluded from inheriting from your parents if they die while you're a minor. If you're named as a beneficiary, you'll receive what is stated in the will. Most likely, some restrictions will apply on large amounts of money or certain valuables. The money may be put into a *trust fund* with instructions that you'll receive part of the fund at certain ages. Property may pass to you through many different arrangements. To help with the business and legal aspects of probate, either the will or a court may appoint an *executor*, or administrator, of the estate.

If you're curious about inheriting from your stepparent, most states don't have laws on the subject. In order for property to pass to you from a stepparent, he or she must have indicated so in a will. Your stepparent can also make a gift of the property to you while alive, thus avoiding the need for a will.

You should also know that property passes both ways—down to you from your parents or anyone else, and up from you to your parents. If you own property and you die intestate, the property will pass to your parents.

"Can I keep what my uncle left me in his will?"

A lot depends on the nature of the bequest, your age, and your level of maturity. For example, if you're nine years old when Uncle Austin leaves you his car, it may sit in the garage for a few years. If you or anyone else isn't harmed or put in danger by the item left to you, then you may have it. Your parents will decide what's best in most situations.

In the movie *Little Big League,* a young boy is left his grandfather's major league baseball team. Anything is possible!

"Do I need a guardian if my parents die?"

A guardian is a person who takes the place of your parents. He or she has the same responsibilities as your mother or father, including caring for you and your social, educational, and medical needs. Likewise, you have an obligation to obey and respect your guardian.

A guardian is either appointed by a court or named by your parents in their will. Usually, a relative or close friend of the family—someone you know—is named as your guardian.

In order for someone to be named a court-appointed guardian, the person must be screened and investigated to determine whether he or she can handle the responsibilities involved. If the court finds that the appointment isn't in your best interests, it won't be made. Another person will then be considered. If no one is available to be your guardian, the state, through Child Protective Services (CPS), will be appointed.

A guardian may be permanent or act as a guardian for you until you turn eighteen. If you get married or are adopted before then, the guardianship ends. In some states, if you're a certain age, you'll have a say in who becomes your guardian. You may have the opportunity to approve or disapprove the guardianship or request a new one. There must be good, sound reasons for the request, or the court will deny it.

Think About It, Talk About It

1. Make a list of the rules you have to follow at home, and think about how they're related to the law.

2. Consider starting a peer support group for teens with common concerns about custody, visitation, and adoption. Invite a local counselor to one of your meetings to discuss some of the issues.

3. You've recently made friends with a new student at your school. One day, she tells you that she's supposed to be living with her mother in another state. Against her mother's wishes, she decided not to return home after visiting her father for the summer. Your friend is afraid of being arrested, pulled out of school, and returned to her mother against her will.

What can you tell her? How can you help?

4. Discuss how you would approach your parents about their rules regarding what you can and can't see at the movie theater, what you're allowed and not allowed to read, or places you're permitted to go.

Chapter 2
You and School

*"It is not enough to have a good mind;
the main thing is to use it well."*
René Descartes, French philosopher

Since the advent of student rights in the 1960s, many on- and off-campus activities have been challenged in the courts. Students have sought and found refuge in the Bill of Rights, with a number of cases getting the attention of the U.S. Supreme Court in Washington, D.C.

Some of your peers have taken a stand regarding incidents at school. As a result, the courts have had to consider your individual rights. For example, the First Amendment guarantees freedom of speech, religion, and the press. When your parents were teenagers, these rights only applied to their parents. Since then, First Amendment protection has been extended to students.

The Fourth Amendment's right to be safe against unreasonable searches and seizures applies to you. The key word here is "unreasonable," as considered in the context of the school setting. Are your locker and backpack private property? Are they off-limits to school security or teachers? What about your car when it's parked on campus? Is a drug test to play sports at school an illegal search?

The Fifth Amendment guarantees of due process and protection against self-incrimination are also on your side. But do you know what the amendment means and how it plays a role in your life? What is due process?

What does the Eighth Amendment's protection against cruel and unusual punishment have to do with you at school? Do you have any recourse if you're unjustly accused of something at school and expelled as a result?

These issues and more are discussed in this chapter. As you read, keep referring to the Bill of Rights below and on page 31. Think about how it applies to your school life. Although the Bill of Rights was written over 200 years ago and amounts to fewer words than one of your homework assignments, it continues to be the foundation of all our rights and a model for democracies around the world.

Bill of Rights—Amendments I to X

I   Congress shall make no law respecting an establishment of religion, or prohibiting the free exercise thereof; or abridging the freedom of speech, or of the press; or the right of the people peaceably to assemble, and to petition the Government for a redress of grievances.

II   A well regulated Militia, being necessary to the security of a free State, the right of the people to keep and bear Arms, shall not be infringed.

III No soldier shall, in time of peace be quartered in any house, without the consent of the Owner, nor in time of war, but in a manner to be prescribed by law.

IV   The right of the people to be secure in their persons, houses, papers and effects, against unreasonable searches and seizures, shall not be violated, and no Warrants shall issue, but upon probable cause, supported by Oath or affirmation, and particularly describing the place to be searched, and the persons or things to be seized.

V   No person shall be held to answer for a capital, or otherwise infamous crime, unless on a presentment or indictment of a Grand Jury, except in cases arising in the land or naval forces, or in the Militia, when in actual service in time of War or in public danger; nor shall any person be subject for the same offence to be twice put in jeopardy of life or limb; nor shall be compelled

"Do I have to go to school?"

By law, all U.S. children are required to go to school. Public education is free, as is transportation to and from school (in most communities), and breakfast and lunch programs are provided for qualifying students. Private school education is also an option, as long as the minimum state law attendance requirements are met.

"Schools function as a marketplace of ideas. . . . The 'robust exchange of ideas' is a special concern of the First Amendment."—U.S. Supreme Court (1967), *Keyishian v. Bd. of Regents*

States differ on the minimum age to begin your education. Some

in any Criminal Case to be a witness against himself; nor be deprived of life, liberty, or property, without due process of law; nor shall private property be taken for public use, without just compensation.

VI   In all criminal prosecutions, the accused shall enjoy the right to a speedy and public trial, by an impartial jury of the State and district wherein the crime shall have been committed, which district shall have been previously ascertained by law, and to be informed of the nature and cause of the accusation; to be confronted with the Witnesses against him; to have compulsory process for obtaining Witnesses in his favor, and to have the Assistance of Counsel for his defence.

VII In suits at common law, where the value in controversy shall exceed twenty dollars, the right of trial by jury shall be preserved, and no fact tried by a jury shall be otherwise re-examined in any Court of the United States, than according to the rules of the common law.

VIII Excessive bail shall not be required, nor excessive fines imposed, nor cruel and unusual punishments inflicted.

IX   The enumeration in the Constitution, of certain rights, shall not be construed to deny or disparage others retained by the people.

X   The powers not delegated to the United States by the Constitution, nor prohibited by it to the States, are reserved to the States respectively, or to the people.

require children who are five or six years old by a certain date (September 1, for example) to begin first grade. The rules vary slightly from state to state; to learn about the law in your state, see the chart on page 180. In most states, parents who fail to send their children to school may be charged with education neglect. Consequences include community service hours, counseling, and/or jail.

There are a few exceptions to the general attendance laws. With the permission of your school district, you may be allowed to study at home. If you're home schooled, you'll be tested on a regular basis to monitor your progress. Some parents are also sending their children to *charter schools*—smaller, specialized programs approved or licensed by the state department of education. In other words, you and your parents are free to decide the nature of your education and where you will attend school.

> Between 1990 and 1996, home schooling doubled to approximately 500,000 students.
>
> **Source:** U.S. Department of Education 1996 Report

Exceptions are made for students who fall into exempt categories, such as actors and actresses. Child labor laws allow young people to work certain hours during the school year,* but the laws specify that their educational needs must be met through a tutor or some other arrangement.

Before starting school or transferring from one school to another, you must be current on all required immunizations. The school will want to see a record of your shots or a letter from your doctor. Most schools have the forms you need to file. If you're not up-to-date on your shots, or if you don't have a doctor, talk with the school nurse or principal. Arrangements may be made with the local health department to give you the needed immunizations. In all states, you're required to be vaccinated against diphtheria, measles, rubella, and polio.

---

* See Chapter 3, pages 55–57.

"How long do I have to stay in school?"

As the chart on page 180 shows, different states have different ages for compulsory school attendance. You can call any school or district office to find out what's required where you live.

If you stop going to school before graduating from high school, you can still earn your diploma. Once you're out of school for six months, you're eligible to enroll in a GED (Graduate Equivalency Diploma) program. When you pass the test and receive your diploma, you'll be able to continue with your education or return to it at a later date.

The law doesn't mandate that you attend a mainstream high school. If your interests lie elsewhere, or your study habits require something other than six hours a day in a classroom, other programs are available. Look into a trade school or vocational program in your area.

Some states have increased the minimum level of education to the twelfth grade. Other states are considering suspending driver's licenses for teens who don't go to

- Although **California** allows kids under 12 one free admission day at citrus fruit fairs, don't make it a school day. It will be counted against you as an unexcused absence.
- Living on an island isn't considered a good enough excuse for missing a day of school in **Massachusetts.** Transportation will be provided for you so you don't miss any days.

school. Generally, you can stay in high school until you graduate. You're not excluded, for example, if you're a sophomore at age eighteen or nineteen. Some states set a maximum age for regular school attendance at twenty-one.

To get high school dropouts involved in education, communities have developed a variety of nontraditional programs. Some help teens with substance abuse issues, while others address teen parenthood or delinquency problems. Project Challenge is a quasi-military federal program sponsored by the National Guard. It's currently in operation in fifteen states: Alaska, Arizona, Arkansas, Georgia, Hawaii, Illinois, Louisiana, Maryland, Mississippi, New Jersey, New York, North Carolina, Oklahoma, Virginia, and West

Virginia. Project Challenge presents a blend of classroom study, community service, and physical training in a seventeen-month program for sixteen- and seventeen-year-old dropouts who are drug-free and not involved with the court.

If a student wants to drop out of North High School in Denver, **Colorado,** the school requires the student and his or her parents to sign a certificate that says: "The undersigned guardian and student accept full responsibility for the listed student being a high school dropout. By signing this disclaimer, I realize that I will not have the necessary skills to survive in the twenty-first century." Most students choose to remain in school and participate in counseling or tutoring programs.

If you're pregnant or have children, you may either finish high school at your regular school, or the district may have a special program for teen mothers. Check with your school counselor for more details.

The National and Community Service Act provides another opportunity to help pay for an education or job training. The program is designed for young people who aren't in school, who have limited English language skills, and/or are homeless or in foster care. You must be between ages sixteen and twenty-five to be considered eligible. Members perform community service work and are paid an allowance of up to $125 per month during the first year. During the second year, members receive up to $200 per month. Check with a high school counselor or your local youth services bureau for information on how to apply.

"What will happen to me if I ditch school?"

State law requires you to be in school for a certain number of days each school year. There is also a maximum number of days allowed for unexcused absences. Once you hit that number, you'll either be suspended for a period of time or expelled. Either consequence is serious and affects your ongoing education and family life.

Thinking About Dropping Out?

Approximately 3,300 young people drop out of school *every day* in the United States. If you've dropped out or are thinking about it, consider these facts:

- 3.8 million persons ages 16–24 were high school dropouts in 1994; of these, 362,000 were ages 16–17.
- During 1994, 498,000 GED credentials were issued, with 35,000 going to persons under age 19.
- Reasons often given for leaving school include not liking school, failing grades, conflicts with teachers, suspension or expulsion, needing a job, and family-related reasons (e.g., pregnancy, etc.).
- The unemployment rate in 1995 among dropouts was 20%, compared to 12% for those who finished high school.

Now consider these average annual salaries (1994 figures):

Less than a ninth grade education:
males	$17,532
females	$12,430

Some high school but no diploma:
males	$22,048
females	$15,133

High school diploma or GED:
males	$28,037
females	$20,373

Two-year college degree:
males	$32,279
females	$23,514

Four-year college degree:
males	$43,663
females	$31,741

Regardless of your reason for leaving or wanting to leave school, there may be a program for teenagers in your same situation. You'll find continuing education programs for teen parents, substance abusers, working teens, and those with poor academic records. Contact a school counselor or district office for information about these opportunities.

Sources: *Digest of Education Statistics 1996*, U.S. Department of Education; *Statistical Abstract of the United States 1996*

Missing school without an acceptable excuse is called *truancy.* Your school's assistant principal or attendance officer may be authorized to issue tickets, order you to appear in court, or even arrest you and take you before a judge if you don't show up for school. The laws differ around the country, but all states have mandatory attendance laws.

- An Alabama mother was arrested in 1996 for not sending her fourth and seventh grade daughters to school. She said she didn't like the school uniforms. She faced 90 days in jail and a $100 fine.
- Two teenagers in Arizona often ditched school because their parents left for work early in the morning and weren't around to supervise. After several warnings by the court, the kids were placed in a foster home for a week while the parents went to jail.

Illness, a death in the family, or other emergencies are reasonable excuses for missing a class or a whole day of school. You may also receive permission to miss school to take a special trip or attend a family function. If possible, let your teacher know in advance about any planned absence.

Schools and courts have become very serious about school attendance. In fact, legislatures are passing laws making parents accountable for their children's truancy. Parents may be fined or jailed if the truancy continues. In Colorado, a fifteen-year-old girl was ordered to spend a month in a detention center for missing forty-three days of school and being late to school nineteen

First semester attendance for U.S. high school seniors (1992):

- 35% missed 3–6 days.
- 26% missed 7 or more days.
- 47% were late for class 3 or more days.
- 24% cut class sometimes.

Source: *Digest of Education Statistics 1996*, U.S. Department of Education

times. Her parents were also sent to jail for ten days and fined $300. A fifteen-year-old girl in South Carolina was *tied to* her mother, by court order, to make sure she went to school and stayed out of trouble.

"Do I have to obey my teacher?"

At the beginning of the school year, you may be given a copy of the school's rules regarding what's expected and the consequences for noncompliance. When you break a school rule, you may face civil or criminal action or both.

Civil action, in the context of school behavior, means the school

> • If you spit at school in **Louisiana,** the penalty is $5 to $25 and 10 days in jail.
> • In **Massachusetts** and **Rhode Island,** spitting at school carries a $20 fine and possible arrest.

may discipline you. It can't lock you up or give you a criminal record, but the consequences may include suspension or expulsion. If what you did also violates the criminal laws of your state, you may be charged with a crime (or delinquent act). This means you'll have to go to court* and may end up on probation. This may seem unfair, since you get punished by the school and again by the court. But this has been determined appropriate, with no violation of your constitutional right against *double jeopardy* (double punishment for the same offense).

If you're sent home, suspended, or expelled for disruptive behavior, your parents will be notified. You're entitled to *due process,* meaning you have a right to be heard. You and your parents may meet with the principal

> "The use of corporal punishment in this country as a means of disciplining school children dates back to the colonial period. . . . Teachers may impose reasonable but not excessive force to discipline a child." —U.S. Supreme Court (1977), *Ingraham v. Wright*

to discuss your behavior and the consequences the school has imposed. This doesn't happen for every infraction—usually only those that carry serious penalties and inclusion in your school record. You may also be entitled to a hearing.

Corporal punishment (swats or paddling) may be permissible in your school, as long as it's not excessive (see the chart on page 181). Physical discipline isn't prohibited by the U.S. Constitution, but it may be limited by state law or school policy. A reasonable amount of force may be used by school officials to break up fights, prevent damage to the school, take weapons from a student, or act in self-defense.

---

* See Chapter 7, pages 137–153.

Courts use the following test to determine if the discipline used at school was reasonable and not cruel or excessive:

- the student's age and maturity
- the student's past behavior
- the instrument used for discipline
- the motivation of the disciplinarian
- the availability of less severe discipline options.

A federal court suggested the following guidelines for school authorities using corporal punishment:

- Students must be given advance notice as to what behavior merits corporal punishment.
- Corporal punishment must not be used for a first offense.
- A second school official must be present when the punishment is carried out.
- A written statement about the incident, punishment, and witnesses must be given to the parent.

It's against the law to insult or abuse your teacher. Because of their special position in the community, teachers are given extra protection under the law. Hitting a teacher is a serious crime (aggravated assault) and carries an increased penalty, including probation, community service hours, fines, and/or time in detention or a state juvenile institution.

School officials are authorized to discipline students for swearing or making obscene statements or gestures. Although you have the right of free expression, it's not without bounds. The U.S. Supreme Court has held that if your activity is "materially and substantially" disruptive to normal school functions, or if you infringe upon the rights of others, restrictions may be imposed. Students should respect *all* school personnel and expect their respect in return.

Unless you're a student, you may not be permitted on school grounds or in a classroom without permission. Interfering with a class may result in charges and penalties for disorderly conduct and trespassing.

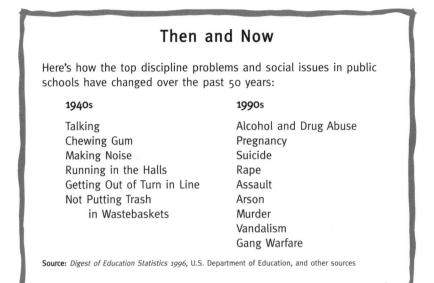

Then and Now

Here's how the top discipline problems and social issues in public schools have changed over the past 50 years:

1940s	1990s
Talking	Alcohol and Drug Abuse
Chewing Gum	Pregnancy
Making Noise	Suicide
Running in the Halls	Rape
Getting Out of Turn in Line	Assault
Not Putting Trash	Arson
in Wastebaskets	Murder
	Vandalism
	Gang Warfare

Source: *Digest of Education Statistics 1996*, U.S. Department of Education, and other sources

"What if I damage school property?"

All students are responsible for taking care of their books and school materials. If yours are damaged or lost, you may have to pay the replacement or repair costs. You'll also have to pay the repair costs of minor acts of vandalism at school, such as a damaged locker, broken window, or graffiti. Stealing or damaging school property may result in suspension or expulsion, as well as having your grades or diploma withheld until the situation is corrected.

- Parents in **Alaska** may be billed up to $2,000 for the acts of their children at school.
- In **Arizona,** parents or guardians are held responsible for all damage done at school by their children.
- In **Iowa,** students are fully responsible for any damage to their school books.

State laws often place financial responsibility on both the student and the parents. There may be a limit on the maximum liability, or the law may be silent on this subject, which means that you and your parents are fully accountable for *all* damage. In 1996, three twelve-year-olds (two girls and one boy) caused $50,000 worth of damage to an elementary school in rural Arizona. They were sentenced to two years probation, 300 hours of community service each, and $1,000 in restitution to cover the school's insurance deductible. The children were also limited to five hours of television time a week while on probation, and they were expelled from their school.

If you damage school property, you may be charged with criminal damage or reckless burning, depending on what you did and how much harm you caused. If someone is injured by your actions, assault or endangerment charges may be filed against you. Intentional or irresponsible conduct at school can result in disciplinary action from both law enforcement and the school.

"Why can't I wear what I want to school?"

Not only has every parent in America been asked this question at one time or other; so have the nine justices of the U.S. Supreme Court. As a result of a decision they made in 1969, you may be attending a school with a dress code, uniforms, or strict rules about T-shirts and protest buttons.

The case was called *Tinker v. Des Moines Independent School District*. During the Vietnam War, a group of parents in Iowa decided to protest the war by wearing black armbands around town during the holiday season. Fearful that the parents' children or other students would do the same, the Des Moines school district passed a policy prohibiting all students from wearing armbands. Any student wearing one to school would be asked to remove it, and if he or she refused, suspension would follow. Three students wore armbands and were suspended, and they took the matter to court.

The Supreme Court crafted a test that still determines whether students' freedom of speech and expression can be restricted. The court emphasized that students are "persons" under the Constitution in school as well as out of school. As persons, their fundamental rights must be respected by the state.

The First Amendment protects not only pure speech but also *symbolic speech,* or nonverbal means of communicating ideas, such as a shirt with a slogan, or a pin or button. Since the armband was a form of symbolic speech, it was protected by the First Amendment. However, the court determined that a student's freedom of expression at school isn't unlimited. If the expression is either "materially or substantially" disruptive to the normal course of events at school, or if it impinges on the rights of others, it may be restricted.

In *Tinker,* the court held that simply wearing a black armband wasn't disruptive to school activities or the rights of other students. This decision opened the door for numerous challenges regarding student activities on campus. As a result, students may not be forced to salute the American flag or recite the Pledge of Allegiance, since these are protected symbols of speech.

Under the *Tinker* test, schools may prohibit certain items of clothing if it can be shown that wearing them is disruptive to the school environment or creates discipline problems. Recently, certain colors, gang insignias, some sports logos, or displays of profanity on clothes have been banned. Generally, if a school's dress code promotes discipline or good health, it will survive a legal challenge.

- A Kentucky eighth grader was suspended from school in 1996 for wearing black lipstick.
- An Ohio middle school has banned baggy, low-slung pants as a safety hazard. Too many boys were tripping at school.

The same principle applies to hairstyles at school. The Supreme Court, in *Olff v. East Side Union High School District* (1972), said, "One's hairstyle, like one's taste for food, or one's liking for certain kinds of music, art, reading, or recreation is certainly fundamental in our constitutional scheme. . . ." However, if a school regulation (such as wearing a hat or hairnet when working in the school cafeteria, or around machinery in metal or wood shop) is related to safety or personal hygiene, it may be upheld as valid.

These rules also apply to private schools if the school receives any federal funding for programs or students. Otherwise, a private school may set its own rules as long as the rules don't discriminate on the basis of race, gender, religion, or nationality.

Aside from the legal arguments about dress and personal appearance, there is also your parents' authority to set the rules. Regardless of what is or isn't allowed at school, if your parents have rules about your appearance or dress, you're expected to follow them.

"Can my property be searched and seized?"

The Fourth Amendment protects you against unreasonable searches and seizures. Does this apply to you at school? Yes. Does it mean that your locker or backpack are off-limits to school personnel? No.

Your school has a responsibility to you and the community to provide you with an education in a safe environment, and to maintain order in the classroom and on campus. This can only be done when problems are kept to a minimum at school. Keeping guns, gangs, drugs, and violence out of schools has become a priority across the nation. Strict rules regarding these activities are legal and enforceable.

A substantial number of sixth- to twelfth-grade students report high levels of violent crime, weapons, and gangs in their schools. Nearly all students are aware of incidents of bullying, physical attack, or robbery at school. Whether as victims or witnesses, students are equally likely to worry about school violence. The Safe Schools Act of 1994 provides funding for conflict resolution and peer mediation programs in schools. The courts have also addressed the issue of safety at school through a number of cases.

The leading case on this subject is *New Jersey v. T.L.O.,* the 1985 U.S. Supreme Court decision that set the standard for school searches. At a New Jersey high school, a teacher caught a freshman girl smoking in the bathroom. The girl was taken to the principal's office, where she denied everything. The assistant principal demanded to see her purse and proceeded to open and search it.

He found a pack of cigarettes, a small amount of marijuana, a marijuana pipe, empty plastic bags, a substantial number of $1 bills, an index card listing students who owed her money, and two letters that suggested she was dealing drugs. When the girl confessed to the police that she had been selling marijuana at school, she was charged and placed on probation.

The court debated whether the search of her purse was a violation of the Fourth Amendment. The court ruled that a school official may conduct a search of a student if there is a "reasonable suspicion" that a crime has been or is in the process of being committed, or that a school rule has been broken. "Reasonable suspicion" means more than a hunch that you're up to something unlawful or are about to break a school rule. Based on a totality of the circumstances—time, place, activity, your school record, age, and source of information—the search may pass the reasonable suspicion test.

Although the court recognized that students have privacy rights at school, these rights are balanced with the school's need to maintain an environment where learning can take place. The court held that the standard to be applied in school searches is that of reasonableness. This covers not only your person, but your locker, desk, car, and backpack. Some cases have extended the search to off-campus incidents, if reasonably related to the school.

Schools are going to great lengths to provide a safe school environment. You may have seen metal detectors and uniformed police officers at your school, on city buses, and at school events. School resource and D.A.R.E. officers are being assigned to

- An 11-year-old South Carolina sixth grader brought a steak knife to school in October, 1996. Although it seemed to be an accident (she was helping her mom pack her lunch), she was suspended from school and charged with possessing a weapon on school grounds. The charge was dropped a few weeks later, and she returned to school.
- In Ohio, 14-year-old Kimberly gave her 13-year-old friend Erica some Midol at school. Kimberly was suspended for 14 days for distributing drugs, and Erica for 9 days for possession. TIP: Give all drugs—including prescription drugs and over-the-counter medications—to your school nurse!

elementary through high schools in a national campaign against drugs and violence at school. Some high schools are using drug-sniffing dogs to randomly check student lockers.

If you find yourself in a search situation at school, the principal and teachers have a right and a duty to question you. When you hear someone say they're "taking the Fifth," this doesn't apply at school unless the police are called in and the person is taken into custody. The "Fifth" here refers to the Fifth Amendment. It means that you don't have to say anything that would help the police charge you with an offense; you have the right to remain silent if charges are filed against you. School officials, however, aren't police officers. They have the authority to investigate school violations, and they can question you.

"Can I be forced to take a drug or urine test if I go out for sports?"

The issue of drug testing at school concerns everyone on campus. While in session, your school is considered to be your temporary guardian. In that capacity, the school exercises a degree of supervision and control over you. This may include a blood or urine test to check for alcohol or drug use.

In addition to offering the standard courses, your school may sponsor a variety of clubs, organizations, and sports. There is no law that automatically entitles you to participate in these activities.

- 25% of students say it's easy to obtain beer, wine, marijuana, or other drugs at school.
- Incidents of physical attack, robbery, and bullying at school increase significantly with the pressure of drug dealers at school.

Source: *Juvenile Offenders and Victims: A National Report,* National Center for Juvenile Justice (1995), with 1996 *Update on Violence*

A student *right* is not the same as a student *privilege.* The school may legally set standards for participation in the activity, including a minimum grade point average, a clean record regarding school infractions, or an initial (and/or random) drug test.

Like many other schools, the Vernonia School District in Oregon adopted a Student Athlete Drug Policy, which authorized random urinalysis drug testing of students who participated in sports. The policy was adopted in the face of increased discipline problems and drug-related injuries to student athletes. The purpose of the policy was to prevent the use of drugs, to protect the students' health and safety, and to provide assistance for avoiding or quitting drugs or alcohol.

In 1991, the District's policy was challenged by a seventh grader who signed up for football but refused to sign the drug-testing consent forms. After a four-year legal battle, the U.S. Supreme Court ruled in support of the policy. In fact, Justice Ruth Bader Ginsburg wrote that consideration should be given to extending the random testing to *all* students, not just athletes. Some schools are using a low-tech version of the police breathalyzer to screen students attending school dances and graduation night parties.

The expectation of privacy that adults enjoy is somewhat lessened for minors in the school setting. There are certain intrusions into your privacy that go along with attending school. These include physical examinations, hearing tests, eye tests, and dental screenings. Student athletes should expect even less privacy due to the nature of school sports—public locker rooms, suiting up together, etc. By choosing to go out for the team, students voluntarily subject themselves to greater regulation than is usually imposed on students.

In applying the reasonableness test, and by balancing the school's interest in a peaceful campus against the limited surrender of a student's privacy, the court determined that random drug testing for athletes is constitutional: "Deterring drug use by our Nation's schoolchildren is . . . important." The results of the tests aren't made public, nor are they sent to the police for criminal prosecution. Deterrence and rehabilitation are the policy's goals.

"Do I have complete freedom of expression in school?"

No one, whether a juvenile or adult (student or not), has *complete* freedom of expression without some limits. The government may place reasonable restrictions on our freedoms. For example, city laws about loud noise at night, dancing in the street, or trespassing after hours in a park have all been found constitutional.

Likewise, students and teachers aren't free to do anything they choose in the name of free speech or expression. Consider this example from U.S. Supreme Court (1988), *Hazelwood School District v. Kuhlmeier:*

> My father "wasn't spending enough time with my mom, my sister, and I" before the divorce—he "was always out of town on business or out late playing cards with the guys" and "always argued about everything."

These statements are from a high school journalism class article about the impact of divorce. Other class articles covered teen pregnancy, sexual activity, and birth control. They were scheduled to be printed in the school newspaper. The principal, thinking that using the student's name in the quoted passage would offend her parents, and that the pregnant teens could be easily identified, withheld the stories from publication. A lawsuit was filed by the newspaper staff, claiming a violation of their First Amendment freedom of expression.

"Students and teachers do not shed their constitutional rights to freedom of speech or expression at the schoolhouse gate." — U.S. Supreme Court (1969), *Tinker v. Des Moines Independent School District*

What do you think? Should the stories have been printed? Should there be a limit on what goes into your school newspaper?

The court ruled that since the paper wasn't a forum for public expression, but would be publicly distributed, the school could exercise control over its content. Teachers are charged with seeing that student activities and personal expression at school are consistent with educational objectives. Offensive, vulgar, or racist expressions may be censored in print, in campaign speeches, and in theater productions.

In a 1996 case, the court spoke of balancing a school's interest in prohibiting profanity with a teacher's interest in using a certain method of teaching creative writing. Cecilia Lacks was a tenured teacher who taught English and journalism at a Missouri high school. One of her assignments was to write and perform short plays. The classroom productions were taped by a school employee. Upon viewing six of the plays and reading two of the students' poems, the school board found that they contained "extensive profanity," which violated school rules. They fired the creative writing teacher. She sued the school district for reinstatement and back wages—and she won.

The court recognized that schools have broad authority to prohibit student profanity. It further stated that it's appropriate to consider the age and sophistication of the students, the relationship between the teaching method and educational objective, and the context and manner of the presentation. Because the context of the offensive language was part of a valid educational objective and not publicly distributed, the court decided it was improper to terminate the teacher. But the court also wrote, "A school must be able to set high standards for the student speech" that is generated at school. Schools may censor expression that is "poorly written . . . biased or prejudiced, vulgar or profane, or unsuitable for immature audiences."

Freedom of Expression: The Right to Speak Out in America by Elaine Pascoe (Millbrook, 1992). Covers political speech, inflammatory speech, flag burning, libel, obscenity, false advertising, speech in the schools, and more. Includes a history of free speech from ancient to modern times.

"Do I have to pray at school?"

In 1989, two prayers were given by a rabbi at a Rhode Island middle school graduation ceremony. Fourteen-year-old Deborah and her father objected to the prayers, but to no avail. School policy permitted principals to invite members of the clergy to offer prayers at graduation ceremonies. Here is one of the prayers Deborah and her father objected to:

> O God, we are grateful to You for having endowed us with the capacity for learning which we have celebrated on this joyous commencement.
>
> Happy families give thanks for seeing their children achieve an important milestone. Send Your blessings upon the teachers and administrators who helped prepare them.
>
> The graduates now need strength and guidance for the future; help them to understand that we are not complete with academic knowledge alone. We must each strive to fulfill what You require of us all: To do justly, to love mercy, to walk humbly.
>
> We give thanks to You, Lord, for keeping us alive, sustaining us, and allowing us to reach this special, happy occasion. AMEN

Deborah challenged the practice as a violation of the Establishment Clause of the First Amendment. The purpose of the Establishment Clause is to maintain a strict separation between church and state. In other words, any government policy or practice must be *secular*—there is to be no state-sponsored religious exercise. States, including public schools, may not advance or inhibit religion, endorse one religion over another, or endorse religion in general. As the U.S. Supreme Court stated in *Lee v. Weisman* (1992), "All creeds must be tolerated and none favored."

Religions may be studied or compared with one another, but public schools may not single out one religion over others to teach or implement its practices. Likewise, public schools may not break for certain holy days over others. As a student, you may observe religious days, such as Yom Kippur, Rosh Hashanah, or Good Friday. These days off from school won't be counted against you as unexcused absences. However, you must make up the work for those days, turn in assignments, and take any missed tests.

"Religious beliefs and religious expression are too precious to be either proscribed or prescribed by the State." —U.S. Supreme Court (1992), *Lee v. Weisman*

The government may not coerce anyone, including students, to support or participate in religious exercises. Nor is it the business of government to compose prayers for any group to recite, or arrange for prayers at a function that students are required or obligated to attend.

Deborah succeeded in her challenge. Although her case was too late to change her middle school graduation, it did affect her high school ceremony. The law applies to every aspect of public school education—classes, assemblies, moments of prayerful silence, and Bible readings. A moment of silent meditation, without any religious overtone, is permissible. Private schools that don't receive federal money don't have these same restrictions.

"Are my grades public information?"

School records, which may include medical, legal, criminal, or mental health information, aren't public records. This means that only certain people have access to them. If you're under eighteen, you may be able to review your records. States and school districts set their own rules regarding access to students' records and transcripts. Once you're eighteen, federal law guarantees you access.

Your parents may view your records upon request. With their permission, usually written, others may be able to see them as well, such as your counselor, psychologist, the police, or a lawyer. Otherwise, the school is required to maintain confidentiality. A *subpoena,* or court order, may also result in disclosure.

When you're a junior or senior in high school and start applying to college or a trade or technical school, you'll take the Scholastic Aptitude Test (SAT), the American College Test (ACT), or similar tests. Your scores will be sent to the schools of your choice and, in turn, those schools will request your high school transcript. You and your parents will need to sign a consent authorizing the release of your records. If you're eighteen, your parents' signature isn't needed.

If, in looking at your high school records, you see something negative or false, you have a remedy. Due process gives you the right to ask the school to remove or correct the statement. If your request is denied, you may *appeal* that decision and ask for a hearing. The appeal process usually starts with the school principal. If you're unsatisfied with his or her decision, you may pursue it further—to the school board, the superintendent, and ultimately to the courts.

If you go to a private school, your rights may be different. Due process under the U.S. Constitution only protects students in public schools. However, most states have laws that provide these protections to private school students as well. Check with your school if you're unsure of your rights. You should be able to obtain a written copy of the school's policies.

"I'm a student with a disability. What rights do I have?"

Not long ago, children with disabilities were excluded from the same educational advantages given to students without disabilities. Beginning in 1975, a number of federal laws were passed by the U.S. Congress that drastically improved the life of children with disabilities. The Education of All Handicapped Children Act of 1975 and the Americans with Disabilities Act of 1990 (ADA) support the basic principle that *all* children are entitled to a "free, appropriate public education." Schools must take a child's disability into consideration in determining his or her needs and how to meet them.

If you're disabled, you're entitled to a complete evaluation to determine your "unique educational needs." Your school is required to develop an Individualized Educational Plan (IEP) designed to allow you to benefit from your education. Your parents may participate in developing this plan. It's reviewed regularly to make sure that it reflects your performance, and it may be adjusted accordingly.

Depending on your IEP, you might be *mainstreamed* into regular classes with the rest of your grade. If you're unable to handle mainstream classes, you may be transferred to a special school or taught at home. The school is required to provide whatever special services are needed to assist with your education, including psychological testing, speech therapy, and medical services. For a state-by-state chart about these special services, see page 182.

For students with disabilities, discipline at school is handled on a case-by-case basis. Your particular disability must be taken into consideration. You may not be suspended for more than ten days or expelled if your behavior is a result of the disability. The law

At an end-of-the-school-year ceremony, 11-year-old J.R. was given three awards: the Pigsty Award, a Procrastinator's Award, and a World's Worst Athlete Award. J.R. is dyslexic (he has a reading disorder) and dysgraphic (he has a writing disorder). He also lacks motor skills. He has received special education since kindergarten.

Were the awards in bad taste, or in the spirit of fun? Is the school responsible for promoting equality among students? Do "joke" awards like these discriminate?

Here's what happened: J.R.'s father sued the school district for discrimination, and a settlement was reached. J.R. received public and private apologies, and the school district had to pay for four years of his college education and his family's attorney's fees.

requires that you be reevaluated to determine if a more restrictive school setting is necessary to meet your educational needs. In other words, you may be removed from the mainstream program and transferred to a special school.

Your attitude and willingness to cooperate with the services offered by your school will be a major factor in your academic and personal success. As disabled actor Christopher Reeve said, "Either you vegetate and look out the window, or activate and try to effect change."

People with Disabilities Resources
http://www.igc.org/pwd/index.html
The Institute for Global Communications' gateway site to hundreds of resources for people with all kinds of disabilities.

"Can I go to school if I have HIV or AIDS?"

Ryan White was thirteen years old when he was diagnosed with the virus that causes AIDS. He had been infected by treatments for his hemophilia. In 1985, he was barred from attending his high school in Indiana because school officials were afraid he might spread the virus to others. The family sued the school district, and in 1986 Ryan won the right to return to school. He learned to drive and, although the disease progressed, he never gave up. He spoke at schools and fund-raisers about misconceptions about AIDS. He died in 1990 at age eighteen. Soon after, Congress passed the Ryan White Comprehensive AIDS Resources Emergency Act of 1990, which funnels millions of dollars into AIDS research, education, and treatment.

School districts have attempted to keep children with HIV and AIDS from going to school. However, once health officials determine that a student presents no danger to others, attendance is approved. Research indicates that casual contact with someone infected with HIV isn't a health risk. If the student's behavior, on the other hand, presents a risk to others (for example, the student has open sores or is prone to biting or fighting with others), he or she may be kept from regular classes, and a special education plan will be developed.

Think About It, Talk About It

1. You have a friend who plays school sports. What would you do if you found out that he or she smokes marijuana over the summer?

2. Would you tell your parents if a younger brother or sister started ditching classes at school? If not, what would you do?

3. Do you feel safe at your school? Would you ever carry a weapon if you felt unsafe at school? What else could you do to protect yourself?

4. Would you like it if you had to wear a uniform to school? Do you think that all schools should require students to wear uniforms? Why or why not?

5. What if you learned that your best friend tested positive for HIV? What would you say? What if other kids at school found out and started to avoid your friend? What would you do?

Chapter 3

You and Your Job

*"U.S. teens, ages twelve to nineteen, spent over
$67 billion of their own money in 1995, and had
a combined income of $102 billion (income from
parents, jobs, and allowance)."*

James McNeal, marketing professor, Texas A&M University

Many teenagers hold down jobs to help support their families,
earn extra spending money, or save for college. You might be
working after school and on weekends, along with your friends
and classmates. How many hours can you legally work while
you're in school? What about curfew? How do you cash your
paycheck? Can you open a bank account? Do you have to pay
taxes now that you're employed? These are natural questions for
any teen who has a job or is thinking of getting one.

This chapter covers a variety of issues about jobs and your legal
rights in the working world. Coworkers, friends, and your parents
may also be able to answer your questions and to give you advice.

"How do labor laws affect me
when I look for work and get a job?"

Guess when this headline appeared: "Grim Report on Child
Labor—200,000 Kids Will Be Hurt on Job This Year."

During the 1800s? Early 1900s? In fact, the above headline
was from a recent report on child labor violations in America (the
American Youth Work Center Report, 1990).

We've come a long way from the days when children worked as many as fifteen hours per day in sweatshop conditions, and today strict federal and state laws exist to protect minors from hazardous jobs. Yet accidents and injuries continue to affect young people at work.

In 1938, Congress passed the Fair Labor Standards Act, which spelled out specific do's and don'ts for employers. The law addresses three areas of child labor: age restrictions, hours of employment, and hazardous jobs. The states have their own child labor laws that, for the most part, shadow the federal law.

If you're a full-time student, much of the law doesn't apply to you, because you're only working after school, on weekends, and during the summer. You don't need to be concerned about employment contracts, unemployment compensation, health insurance, or other long-term benefits. Once you graduate from high school or college and join the workforce full-time, however, these issues will be important to you.

Unless you're eighteen, a number of jobs will be off-limits to you. These include logging, railroading, and mining. You also can't work with power-driven machinery, dynamite, dangerous chemicals, and radioactive materials. Once you're eighteen, you may work anywhere and for any length of time.

States may also have limits on other hazardous and non-hazardous jobs. In some cases, the age restrictions are lowered. For example, you may deliver papers, bag groceries, or wait tables at a younger age. You may work in a family business before you're eighteen. If your family owns a farm, you may be restricted from operating certain equipment until you're sixteen or eighteen. Cities and towns have also begun restricting door-to-door sales by minors (to a minimum age and between certain hours).

In addition to age restrictions, prohibited job categories, and limits on working conditions, there are rules about the number of hours you can work. These include:

- no school hours
- when school is out, no more than forty hours per week, and only eight hours each day
- when school is in session, no more than eighteen hours per week, and only three hours each day
- during the school year, between 7:00 A.M. and 7:00 P.M.; in the summer (June 1 to Labor Day) to 9:00 P.M.

If you're considering a job that's a little out of the ordinary or has unusual hours, check the library for your state's labor laws. They vary among the states and may not follow the federal law described above. In fact, your state may have stricter laws regarding certain jobs. You'll need a social security number and possibly a work permit or employment certificate before you start your job. Your employer will let you know if a permit is required.

- In **Florida,** you must be 16 before you can wrestle an alligator.
- If you're 11 or 12, you may work as a golf caddie for eighteen holes each day in **Kentucky.**
- In **Massachusetts,** you must be 18 to get a license to perform as a contortionist.
- In **New York,** you must be 17 to get hired as a cigar stump collector, rag picker, or bone collector.
- If you want to harvest wild rice in **Wisconsin,** you have to wait until you're 16, but there's no age limit in **Washington** if you want to pick berries after school.

Can you be fired for no reason? In most cases, the answer is yes. Unless you have a contract with your employer, you're considered an *employee-at-will.* This means you work at the pleasure of your boss, and your boss can let you go for any reason.

Employers may not discriminate against you on the basis of disability, race, color, gender, or religion. The Civil Rights Act of 1964 and the Americans with Disabilities Act of 1990 (ADA) protect you from unlawful discrimination. Recognizing that there are 43 million Americans with physical and mental disabilities, the U.S. Congress intended the ADA to provide a clear mandate for the elimination of discrimination against individuals with disabilities.

The ADA requires equality of opportunity and treatment for persons with disabilities in private and public employment. It also applies to services offered by state and local governments, and places of public accommodation. The ADA covers employers with at least fifteen employees, so it may not apply to you. The Act doesn't guarantee your position; it only requires employers to reasonably accommodate your disability regarding work schedule, job assignment, and the purchase of specialized equipment. If accommodation creates an undue hardship on the employer, the Act doesn't apply.

The law, however, doesn't require employers to hire you. You still must qualify for any job, and you must be able to do the work once you start. If you believe that you have been discriminated against at work or in applying for a job, do something about it! First, discuss your concerns with the employer. You may want to tell your parents and see if they can assist you in resolving the problem. If these steps are unsuccessful, contact the local office of the Equal Employment Opportunity Commission (EEOC) to review your case and help resolve it.

Kid Cash: Creative Money-Making Ideas by Joe Lamancusa (Tab Books, 1993). Dozens of concrete, creative suggestions for earning money, samples of advertising flyers, and tips on what to charge for your services, how to keep records, and how to handle your profits. Written by a fourteen-year-old with firsthand experience running his own business.

Summer Jobs for Students (Peterson's Career Focus Books, 1997). Covers all types of summer jobs (camp counselors, lifeguards, wilderness guides, summer theater stagehands, clerical positions, etc.), gives suggestions for applying, lists contact persons, and includes salary information about positions throughout the U.S. and Canada.

"What are my rights as a working teenager?"

You may feel that you have few rights as a teenager, and even fewer while at work. You get the worst hours (usually Friday and Saturday nights), the dirtiest assignments (cleanup!), you have to wear a ridiculous shirt and hat—and all for minimum wage. In spite of this bleak picture, you and adults have almost the same rights on the job.

One of your most important rights is the protection you have against discrimination. This means that it's against the law for any employer to hire, fire, promote, or pay you based on your religion, race, gender, color, or disability. Your qualifications and job performance are the only valid factors to be considered in evaluating you. The Civil Rights Act of 1964 assures you of these protections, and the law applies to teenagers as well as adults.

Due to federal and state laws about child labor (see pages 55–58), you may be restricted from certain jobs due to your age. This may be a form of discrimination, but it's not illegal. Since most teenagers work only part-time, they don't qualify for health insurance, paid vacation, sick leave, and retirement plans. As a part-time employee, however, you're entitled to a safe workplace, and possibly worker's compensation if you get injured on the job. This would assist you with medical bills and lost time at work.

As a full- or part-time employee, you may also be drug tested or searched by your employer. It's the employer's responsibility to maintain a safe workplace. If you're suspected of alcohol or drug use, a reasonable search at work is permissible. You may also be subjected to a dress code while at work. It's not discriminatory or illegal if the business requires a uniform or prohibits tattoos or certain hairstyles. Your personal appearance is important to any business, particularly those that serve the public.

Whether you're single or married, your employer can't fire you if you become pregnant. The same is true if you have an abortion.

If you've worked full-time for at least one year, you're entitled to maternity leave under the Family and Medical Leave Act of 1993. Although there's no guarantee that you'll be paid during your leave, you won't lose your job because of your absence. This applies to mothers and fathers alike.

The Family and Medical Leave Act also allows eligible employees to take up to twelve weeks of unpaid leave for childbirth, adoption, or the placement of a foster child in the home. It also applies when providing for the care of a spouse, child, or parent with a serious medical condition, or your own medical care. Most teenagers don't qualify, since eligibility requires one year of employment, with at least 1,250 hours worked that year. The Act applies to employers of more than fifty employees, which also eliminates a number of teen parents.

If you believe that you've been illegally discriminated against by your employer, take action! First, talk with your parents. They may suggest a meeting with your employer to attempt to work things out. If this is unsuccessful, you may want to contact a lawyer with a background in employment law. You can also register a complaint with the Equal Employment Opportunity Commission (EEOC) or, as a last resort, file a lawsuit. You have rights and the responsibility to assert them, so don't be afraid to stand up for yourself.

"What do I put on a job application if I'm asked about prior arrests?"

You should write the truth. The exact phrasing of the question on the application is important. There's a difference between being *arrested* for a crime and being *convicted* of a crime. You may be arrested by the police, with no further action taken. If you're not charged with a crime and are released from custody, the arrest may remain on your record. This means that the arrest may show up in a computer check with local police or through the FBI.

If you answer no on a job application when, in fact, you *were* arrested, you'll have to explain the situation. Employers are reluctant to hire someone who isn't straightforward and honest. After indicating that you were arrested, you might further volunteer that charges were never filed or that an error was made. Explain in a short statement whatever happened at the time of the incident.

- Over 2.7 million persons under 18 were arrested in 1994—45% were boys, and 25% were girls ages 16 and 17.
- 35% of juveniles arrested in 1994 were under age 15. Most of them were arrested for arson, vandalism, theft, running away, assault, and burglary.

Source: *Juvenile Offenders and Victims: A National Report*, National Center for Juvenile Justice (1995), with 1996 *Update on Violence*

On the other hand, the question on the application might be whether you've ever been *convicted* of a crime. There's no getting around the question—either you were convicted (found guilty of the charge) or you weren't convicted (found innocent of the charge). Simply answer the question. If you feel an explanation should be made, add a brief statement.

Having a record may prevent you from getting certain jobs. Depending on the type of job and the nature of your record, an employer can legally decline to hire you. For example, if you have two speeding tickets and you apply to be a messenger for a local company, you're not likely to get the job because of insurance restrictions. Once you're hired for a job, however, you qualify for certain rights and can't be discriminated against, as explained in the preceding question.

"If I work, will I be making minimum wage?"

The Fair Labor Standards Act establishes an hourly minimum wage for the U.S. workforce. When the Act was passed in 1938, the minimum wage was twenty-five cents per hour. Currently, minimum wage is $5.15 per hour. If you're under age twenty, you may be paid $4.25 per hour for the first three months, as a training wage for new employees.

States may also set minimum wages that employers must pay. What you're paid depends on the job and your employer, whether you work in a private business or a government office. Some jobs—including professional positions like doctors, architects, and professors—are exempt from the minimum wage.

Here's how the minimum wage has changed over the years:

1950	$0.75
1970	$1.45
1980	$3.10
1990	$3.80
1996	$4.25
1997	$5.15

If you're a restaurant server, you may have been surprised at your first paycheck. If you did the math in your head before getting paid, your figure was probably higher than the check. This is because your tips may be considered as wages. If you make more than $30 in tips each month, your boss may pay you less than the minimum wage.

Can a worker be paid for overtime hours? Yes. For every hour an employee works over forty hours each week, the law requires that you be paid "time-and-a-half," which is one and a half times the employee's regular hourly rate. This may not apply to you or your friends, because most teens work less than forty hours each week. The law, in fact, limits you to less than forty hours per week while you're in school.

"Do I have to pay income taxes?"

Given the size of your paycheck, you may think that you don't have to worry about taxes. "How could I owe income tax on the peanuts I earn?" Well, neither the federal government nor state governments feel this way. If you earn *any* amount of money throughout the year, you may have to pay a tax to either the state or federal government, or both.

State income tax laws differ, so you'll have to check the rules where you live. Some states have no income tax. The federal tax laws apply to everyone who earns an income. If you earn $6,400 during the year (January through December), you're required to file with the federal government's Internal Revenue Service (IRS). Most teens working part-time don't earn this much.

You may, however, want to file an income tax return in order to claim a refund of any amounts withheld from your check by your employer. While you work, your employer may withhold part of your paycheck. This adds up over the course of the year. When you do your taxes, you'll either owe the government or receive a refund. If you overpaid (too much withholding), you'll get the difference back. If you underpaid, you'll owe the difference, which is due by April 15 of each year.

State and federal tax forms come with instructions, but talk with your parents before you try to fill out the forms. Tax laws are complicated, and it's easy to make a mistake. If you have to file, you'll probably use the "EZ" form (unless you're married or your income was over the stated amount on the form). As you continue to work and your income increases, you may want to consult with a tax service or accountant for assistance.

Federal tax information is available from the IRS 24 hours a day, 7 days a week. To find the number in your area, contact your local IRS office or look in a tax form instruction booklet (available at many government offices, post offices, banks, and libraries).

Most teenagers qualify for a new service called TeleFile, where you can do everything by telephone. Once you have your paperwork in order, use a touch-tone phone and call toll-free 1-800-829-5166. Follow the instructions and you're done until next year. The whole process takes about five minutes and, if you're receiving a refund, it should arrive within three weeks.

You can download tax forms and instructions from the IRS Web site: *http://www.irs.ustreas.gov/*

"Can I open my own bank account?"

Between expenses for transportation, personal items, and entertainment, you may be living from paycheck to paycheck. But if you're in the habit of setting $5 or $10 aside each payday, you might want to consider opening your own bank account. Ask your parents for advice on this—if you live at home, you're still subject to their rules. Unless you're emancipated,* your parents can decide what you do with your money, including how much you can keep, what you can spend it on, and how much goes into the bank.

- Kids in a number of states, including **Ohio, Pennsylvania,** and **South Carolina,** may open bank accounts and withdraw and deposit money without a parent's consent.
- A 1996 study indicated that 66% of teens have savings accounts, 20% have checking accounts, and 17% own stocks or bonds.

Source: Teenage Research Unlimited, Northbrook, IL

Some banks offer special savings programs to students, or they waive their monthly service fees for minors with accounts. This could save you anywhere from $5 to $100 each year. Also, find out what interest rate the bank pays on a savings account. Most banks are within a fraction of a percent of each other, but shopping around may be to your advantage.

A checking account may be a good way to keep a record of your expenses. It's also safer than carrying around a large amount of cash. Some checking accounts pay you interest, while others charge monthly fees for certain transactions. There may be a fee for going into the bank and dealing with a teller or using the automatic teller machine (ATM)

- Studies in 1996 indicated that children ages 4–12 earned or received $20 billion in 1995, and those ages 12–19 earned or received $67 billion, from work, allowance, and gifts. The money was spent on food and beverages, toys, movies, sports, and video arcades.
- Teens average 3 trips to the mall each month, spending an average of $41 each time on clothes.

Sources: Associated Press report dated 4/25/96 of a study from Texas A&M University; Teenage Research Unlimited, Northbrook, IL

---

* See Chapter 5, pages 96–98.

outside the bank. Make sure you find out about all of the fees the bank charges for your type of account. Fees can add up quickly, and you may lose any benefits of having the account.

When you open up a bank account, check your monthly statement for accuracy, and learn how to balance your checkbook. Banks occasionally make mistakes, and these should be brought to their attention immediately. As the amount of money in your account increases, consider investing in stocks, bonds, or mutual funds—this is a good way to help your money to grow. You'll need your parents' consent and a social security number to make an investment.

The Kids' Guide to Money: Earning It, Saving It, Spending It, Growing It, Sharing It by Steve Otfinoski (Scholastic, 1996). How to earn money, save for a big purchase, understand the stock market, choose a worthy cause for charity, avoid getting ripped off, and more.

"Can I start my own business?"

The general answer is yes. Because many employers won't hire anyone younger than fifteen or sixteen, entrepreneurial teens have found that starting a business is a great way to join the workforce and earn money.

Before starting a business, research the laws in your state regarding businesses owned by minors. Not only do state laws differ, but cities also have their own requirements for retail and service businesses. You may have to get a license to conduct your business, as well as a tax number from your city and state so you can report your earnings and pay the appropriate taxes.

If you aren't eighteen, a parent or guardian will be required to co-sign any papers you need to start your new business. Also, your earnings from the business may not, under your state laws, be entirely yours to keep. Your parents are legally responsible for you until you're eighteen (or until you're emancipated).* This means that your parents may control your income or help you to save some of it.

FYI

Better than a Lemonade Stand: Small Business Ideas for Kids by Daryl Bernstein (Beyond Words Publishing, Inc., 1992). Describes dozens of money-making ventures including curb address painter, birthday party planner, disc jockey, dog walker, house checker, newsletter publisher, photographer, and sign maker. Daryl was fifteen years old when he wrote and published this book.

Girls and Young Women Entrepreneurs: True Stories About Starting and Running a Business Plus How You Can Do It Yourself (Free Spirit Publishing, 1997). Not just for girls and young women, this book inspires all young people to think like entrepreneurs, be creative, take positive risks, identify their interests, strengthen their talents and abilities, and focus on their futures. Includes first-person stories, advice, and insights, step-by-step instructions on how to develop an idea into a business, up-to-date information about groups to contact, a chronology of women in business, and helpful resources.

The Totally Awesome Business Book for Kids—And Their Parents by Arthur Berg Bochner and Adriane G. Berg (Newmarket Press, 1996). A financial expert and her twelve-year-old son suggest twenty super businesses for kids ages ten to seventeen, with special attention to jobs that help the environment.

---

* See Chapter 5, pages 96–98.

Think About It, Talk About It

1. Last summer you started your own lawn maintenance business, and you did pretty well. You plan to expand this year and need to hire a helper.

As a boss, do you have to follow all of the labor laws? What should you pay your help, and what if he or she doesn't do the job right?

2. You're a server at a restaurant and you like your job, but you have a few questions. Your first paycheck was a surprise—it was short almost $40—and the other employees told you that the boss deducts for broken dishes, misorders, and unpaid checks.

What should you do? You're only making $2 per hour plus tips. Do you have to put up with these rules?

3. You opened up a checking account last year, and things went okay until recently. You've been writing out checks and overdrawing your account by about $10 (sometimes more, sometimes less). You've had three overdrafts in the past three months, and your mother is threatening to close your account.

What should you do?

Chapter 4

You and Your Body

*"We all have the power of choice, but once used,
our choice has power over us.
Weigh the consequences of your decisions."*
NBA All-Star A.C. Green

It's your life, and how you live it is your decision. This chapter will help prepare you for the consequences of personal decisions and privacy rights as they affect your body, health, and physical well-being. As a teen, you'll be making many choices, some of which involve health and hygiene issues, sexual behavior, disease or disability, and your overall right to privacy.

Your right to privacy extends to marriage, having children, birth control, family relationships, and education. Teenagers often have a lot of questions when it comes to their health and physical well-being. They wonder about their rights to seek medical care, and whether birth control, abortions, and substance abuse counseling are available to them without parental consent.

These and other personal issues are important to you, your family, and your friends. Even if the situations described in this chapter don't apply specifically to you, you may know someone who needs help. The more you know about your rights, the better equipped you'll be to help yourself and others.

"Can I go to the doctor without my parents' permission?"

Most doctors, health care professionals, and hospitals require written permission from your parents or legal guardian before seeing you. There are, however, some exceptions to this rule.

The first is called *medical neglect*. Since your parents are responsible for your care, if they refuse to take you to the doctor, or if they fail to give you medicine that your doctor has prescribed, the state may step in and see that your medical needs are met. If you, a sibling, or a friend is a victim of medical neglect, it should be reported to Child Protective Services (CPS). If there's a risk of bodily harm or injury, or someone's life is in danger, the state will get involved. When you call CPS, ask to speak with a social worker and fully explain the situation.

If you're under eighteen and don't live at home, you may be able to obtain medical care without your parents' consent. You're allowed to go to the doctor on your own, for example, if you're emancipated (legally free) under the laws of your state,* or if you're married or a parent. You can arrange for your own health care if you're pregnant or were sexually assaulted—whether your parents know about your circumstances or not.

If your parents are unavailable in an emergency situation and you need medical care or surgery, health care professionals may treat you. If your parents are going out of town, they should leave written consent for the person you're staying with to take you to the doctor if necessary.

Due to an increase in substance abuse by young people, a number of states have lowered the age for treatment and counseling without parental consent. In some states, a twelve-year-old may independently obtain alcohol and drug counseling. If you're in a treatment program under these circumstances, your identity is kept confidential and is disclosed to others only with your consent.

---

* See Chapter 5, pages 96–98.

Teenagers can also receive health care on their own for the diagnosis and treatment of sexually transmitted diseases (STDs) such as herpes, gonorrhea, and syphilis. In most parts of the country, you have these same rights regarding diagnosis for HIV and AIDS. At very little or no cost, you may go to a clinic for diagnosis and counseling. Some family planning clinics, for example, charge $20 for an HIV/STD test and counseling. The cost for treatment may also be on a sliding scale basis, or you may be eligible for public assistance.

For specific information on the laws in your state about seeking medical care, contact your library, health department, or family doctor. Check out the issue of costs for health care. Who is legally responsible for your bills if you seek treatment without your parents' consent? Find this out in advance! The number for your local public health agency is in the white pages of your telephone directory, or ask directory assistance for help.

AIDS: Answers to Questions Kids Ask by Barbara Christie-Dever (Learning Works, 1996). Questions and answers about the risks and dangers of infection, activities to increase AIDS awareness and develop skills in saying no, and biographical sketches of Ryan White, Magic Johnson, and others.

Coping When You or a Friend is HIV-Positive by Pat Kelly (Rosen Publishing Group, 1995). What to say and do.

Everything You Need to Know About STDs by Samuel Woods, Jr. (Rosen Publishing Group, 1994). Facts and figures about sexually transmitted diseases, information about causes and prevention, and sound advice about risky behavior that makes teens vulnerable.

Living in a World with AIDS by Anna Forbes (Rosen Publishing Group, 1996). An introduction to AIDS, how people become infected, and how to avoid infection.

American Red Cross HIV/AIDS Teen Hotline

1-800-440-8336

http://www.redcross.org/

The Red Cross offers a peer-to-peer HIV/AIDS education program. Peer counselors are available Fridays and Saturdays from 6:00 P.M.– 12:00 A.M. EST to help in times of crisis by offering information and referral services. Contact your local office to learn how to become a peer counselor.

The Body: A Multimedia AIDS and HIV Information Resource

http://www.thebody.com/

Information, resources, support organizations, hotlines, insight from experts, forums for connecting with others, and *much* more. A comprehensive, up-to-the-minute site.

In Our Own Words: Teens & Aids

http://www.abouthealth.com/teens/teens.html

Kerry, Pedro, David, and other teens describe what it's like to live with AIDS.

National HIV/AIDS Hotline

1-800-342-AIDS (1-800-342-2437)

Spanish: 1-800-344-SIDA (1-800-344-7432)

TTY: 1-800-AIDS-TTY (1-800-234-7889)

Confidential 24-hour information and referral hotline sponsored by the Centers for Disease Control (CDC)

National STD Hotline

1-800-227-8922

Information and referral hotline sponsored by the Centers for Disease Control (CDC).

Teenagers & HIV/AIDS

http://www.HIVpositive.com/

Click on "Women & Children," then scroll down the menu on that page and click on "Teenagers & HIV/AIDS" to find facts about teens with HIV/AIDS, information about prevention and education programs, and a guide to resources. Part of the large HIVpositive.com™ site.

Teens Teaching AIDS Prevention (Teens TAP)

1-800-234-8336

Trained teens answer questions about HIV/AIDS and other STDs. Mondays– Fridays, 4:00 P.M.–8:00 P.M., closed on national holidays. Backed by the Good Samaritan Project.

"Can I donate my blood and organs?"

Generally, you can't give blood until you're eighteen. Once you're an adult, the decision is yours. A few states allow younger teens to donate blood, with written consent from their parents and/or a doctor.

You might also have to satisfy certain health and minimum weight requirements before you're allowed to donate. For example, the American Red Cross requires you to be seventeen (in states where the limit is seventeen) and weigh 110 pounds. If you're HIV-positive, they won't accept your donation. It's always best to check with your family doctor if you have any concerns. Discuss your thoughts and plans with your parents, too.

Although some blood banks pay donors each time they come in, teens are generally not eligible. If you're emancipated* and your state law permits payment to minors, you can keep the payment. If you're not emancipated, your parents have a say about any money you earn or receive.

You also may donate your organs when you die. If you're eighteen, you may advise the National Kidney Foundation, for example, that you wish to be a kidney donor. When you apply for your driver's license, there's a question regarding organ donation, and your donor status is marked on your license.

American Red Cross
1-800-272-0024
http://www.redcross.org/
Information about being a blood donor. Or contact your local blood bank or plasma center. Many blood centers also have information about organ and tissue donations.

---

* See Chapter 5, pages 96–98.

"What can I do if I'm being abused or neglected?"

The abuse and neglect of children in the United States is epidemic. Approximately 3 *million* reports of child abuse and neglect are made each year. Three children die every day at the hands of their parents or caretakers.

Abuse may be:

- physical (acts that cause physical injury)
- sexual (sexual activity that provides gratification or financial benefit to the *perpetrator,* or the person committing the abuse, such as sexual conduct, prostitution, pornography, or sexual exploitation), or
- emotional (acts or omissions that cause mental disorders in a child).

Neglect may be:

- physical (including abandonment and/or failure to provide supervision, health care, adequate food, clothing, or shelter)
- emotional (including inadequate nurturance, or a disregard for a child's emotional or developmental needs), or
- educational (including permitting chronic truancy or otherwise disregarding the child's educational needs).

When two young Illinois girls (ages 4 and 9) were left home alone for a week at Christmas while their parents vacationed in Mexico, the parents were charged with neglect. The parents were sentenced to 2 years probation and 200 hours of community service. Several months later, they gave up the girls for adoption.

Child abuse and neglect are against the law. If you witness or hear about an incident of abuse or neglect, you should report it to the police or Child Protective Services (CPS). Every state has mandatory reporting laws spelling out the legal obligations of teachers, doctors, social workers, and anyone responsible for children. An adult who fails to report suspected abuse or neglect of a child has violated the law.

CPS is an agency of state government charged with the duty to investigate abuse, neglect, and abandonment cases. In most states, CPS provides services to families to help them to solve their problems and stay together. For example, parents may discipline their child, but if the punishments are excessive, leaving welts or bruises, the police and courts may get involved to protect the child. If a child is removed from the home and placed in foster care, services are offered to assist in reuniting the family. If the parents are unsuccessful in their efforts, or if they refuse to cooperate, the child may stay with relatives or remain in foster care or an adoptive home.

- Neglect is the most common form of child maltreatment, affecting 50% of abuse victims.
- 53% of reported child abuse victims are female.
- Approximately 40% of abuse victims are between ages 9–17.
- There were 1,028 known deaths of abuse and neglect victims in 1993, and 1,111 reported deaths in 1994.

Sources: *Juvenile Offenders and Victims: A National Report,* National Center for Juvenile Justice (1995), with 1996 *Update on Violence; Child Maltreatment 1994: Reports from the States to the National Center on Child Abuse and Neglect,* U.S. Department of Health and Human Services (1996)

If you're in danger, or you know someone who's injured or has been abused at home, tell someone you trust. A teacher, school nurse, or police officer will be able to offer assistance. If a friend tells you that he or she has been sexually molested, tell a responsible adult. You're protected under the law when reporting suspected abuse or neglect. As long as you're truthful in reporting, the law protects you from being sued. You may also report anonymously (without giving your name), although identifying yourself might help the investigation.

Coping with Family Violence by Morton L. Kurland, M.D. (Rosen Publishing Group, 1990). Drugs, economic and emotional stress, and broken homes are some of the causes for the rise in child abuse. This book tells abused teens how to alleviate some of the pain and suffering they feel.

CHILDHELP USA Child Abuse Hotline
1-800-4-A-CHILD (1-800-422-4453)
Crisis counseling, referrals, information, and support for U.S. and
Canadian teens, children, and adult survivors.

National Child Abuse Hotline
1-800-25ABUSE (1-800-252-2873)

National Clearinghouse on Child Abuse and Neglect Information
1-800-394-3366
Referrals and resource information, sponsored by the U.S. Department of
Public Health.

National Domestic Violence/Abuse Hotline
1-800-799-SAFE (1-800-799-7233)
TTY/TDD: 1-800-787-3224
Callers can be connected directly to help in their communities, including
emergency services and shelters, as well as receive information and referrals, counseling and assistance in reporting abuse. Calls to the hotline
are confidential, and callers may remain anonymous if they wish.

"Can I get birth control?"

If you choose to be sexually active, it's important to know your
rights regarding birth control. Strictly speaking, yes, you can get
birth control. Regardless of your age, the law allows you to obtain
birth control, whether prescription or nonprescription. Condoms,
foam, and spermicidal gels are available from a drugstore, phar-
macy, or grocery store without a prescription. With a doctor's prescription, you can get birth control pills, an IUD or a diaphragm,
or Norplant.

The law doesn't require your
parents' consent for birth control.
Public health agencies (many are
based in county or city hospitals)
or family planning clinics may be
able to assist you. Costs vary from
no fee to sliding scale fees, depending on your income, or you may be
charged higher amounts based on
the services you use.

- Over 1,400 babies are born to teenage mothers every day in the U.S.
- A study in *American Journal of Public Health* (April 1996) found that 66% of teen mothers ages 11 and up had children from fathers over age 20.
- 27% of U.S. females drop out of school because of pregnancy.

Sources: *The State of America's Children Yearbook 1997,* Children's Defense Fund; *Juvenile Offenders and Victims: A National Report,* National Center for Juvenile Justice (1995), with 1996 *Update on Violence*

If you're sexually active, be aware of the consequences of unsafe sex and pregnancy. Unless you're married and want a child, contact a local clinic or agency for information and counseling. If the agency receives federal money for family planning services, it's required by law to maintain your confidentiality. Planned Parenthood is one such agency. When first contacting the agency, feel free to ask about their policies regarding your privacy rights.

Your school may offer sex education classes. Although you can't be forced or required to take such a class, learning the facts about sex from a well-balanced presentation can help you to make intelligent decisions about sex. Discuss the sex education class option with your parents. Perhaps you can review an outline of the course before deciding whether to take it.

Coping with Birth Control by Michael D. Benson, M.D. (Rosen Publishing Group, 1997). Precise birth control information so teens can make intelligent decisions.

Planned Parenthood Federation of America
http://www.plannedparenthood.org/
Extensive information resources on sexuality, pregnancy, STDs, HIV, etc., with many links to other sites.

The Safer Sex Page
http://safersex.org/
Everything you want and need to know about AIDS, birth control, and sexual health. Includes discussion forums. NOTE: This site contains explicit material.

"Can I get an abortion without telling my parents?"

In 1973, Justice Harry Blackmun wrote the majority opinion for the U.S. Supreme Court in *Roe v. Wade*, the now famous abortion decision. He wrote that the Fourteenth Amendment's protection of liberty is broad enough to include a woman's decision regarding her pregnancy: "[T]he right of personal privacy includes the abortion decision . . . but . . . this right is not unqualified."

The court balanced your right to privacy against the state's interest in protecting a *viable fetus*—a fetus that could survive outside of its mother before natural birth. Consequently, during the first trimester of pregnancy (approximately twelve weeks after conception) you may obtain an abortion. During the second trimester, states may impose restrictions regarding the life and health of the mother; during the final trimester, states may prohibit abortion altogether.

In a later case, these abortion rights were extended to teen mothers. Whether you're single, married, separated, or divorced—regardless of your age—you may get an abortion.

- In 1991, 12,000 abortions were performed on girls ages 14 and under.
- Young women ages 15–19 had 314,000 abortions.

Source: *Statistical Abstract of the United States 1996,* U.S. Department of Commerce

The issue of parental consent has also been raised and decided. A state may require either a parent or a court to consent to a minor's abortion. In requiring a parent's consent or notification, the law must also include what is called a *judicial bypass* procedure. If a parent refuses to give consent, or if notifying the parent would endanger the minor, the parent may be bypassed and consent obtained from a court. In other words, neither your parents nor the father of the child has absolute veto power over your decision. Nor can your parents force you to have an abortion. Your privacy rights allow you to make the final decision.

Under the appropriate circumstances, you may petition the court directly for its consent. The judge will meet with you and possibly your lawyer (if one has been assigned to represent you) to discuss the situation. You may also have a counselor with you. It's the court's job to make sure you understand the decision to abort, and that you have received counseling regarding the alternatives to abortion. Even if the judge finds that you lack the maturity to make an intelligent decision, consent may still be given based on what's in your best interests.

Before making a decision, take time to learn about your options. Talk with someone you trust. If you decide against abortion, contact a local family planning agency to get information about foster care and adoption. You have the right to keep your child, sometimes with the help of the state (depending on your age), just as you have the right to place your child for adoption.* Consider *all* of your options before deciding what to do.

Abortion: Understanding the Controversy by Joann Bren Guernsey (Lerner Publications Co., 1993). Presents opposing viewpoints on abortion, discussing its biological, medical, and legal aspects.

Planned Parenthood Locator Service
1-800-230-7526
Call this number to reach the Planned Parenthood office nearest you. They offer counseling on birth control, abortion, alternative placement options (foster care and adoption), and more. The service is free and confidential; parental consent isn't required. A translator service is also provided.

"What is date rape, and what can I do to protect myself?"

"Was it rape?" "I told him no, but he wouldn't stop!" "I had a few drinks and let my guard down." "I've known him for years—I thought he respected me." These are common statements of rape and date rape victims. Due to a

Rape statistics from the latest reporting year (1994) show that:

- 6,000 juveniles were arrested for forcible rape.
- 38% were under age 15.
- 43% were ages 16–17.

Source: *Juvenile Offenders and Victims: A National Report,* National Center for Juvenile Justice (1995)

---

* See Chapter 1, pages 6–8.

few well-publicized cases, people have become more aware of incidents of date or acquaintance rape. Yet date rape continues to increase in frequency and remains underreported.

Rape means having sexual intercourse with a male or female forcibly and without his or her consent. Rape can occur among a male and a female or two people of the same gender; either a male or a female may commit the rape. In gang rape, a person is raped by several different people. Annual reports indicate that 20 to 25 percent of U.S. women are victims of rape or attempted rape. Five percent of rapes result in pregnancy, or 32,000 unwanted pregnancies each year.

It may also be considered rape, and therefore a crime, if both parties consent to sex but one person is under a certain age. Some states have established a minimum age before a girl can legally consent to having intercourse. If you have sex with someone under the legal age limit, even if it's with the consent of the underage person, you've broken the law. A violation is referred to as *statutory rape,* which is a felony. If the victim is injured, or the incident involves a weapon, threats, or violence, the act becomes *aggravated rape,* which carries a greater penalty.

In cases of date rape, victims usually know their offenders. The offender can be a longtime friend or casual acquaintance. Drugs and alcohol are major contributors to date rapes. Some experts suspect that only one out of ten date rapes is reported. Because of low reporting, and the even lower incidence of prosecution and conviction, education may be the only way to deal with date rape.

Many high schools and colleges offer orientation programs aimed at rape awareness and prevention. Fraternities and sororities are conducting similar programs. They advise students to always be on the alert, to walk with friends at night, and to carry pepper spray, mace, or a whistle. Students are also warned to remain sober to lessen the risk of date rape.

If you're a victim of rape, date rape, or a rape attempt, *get help.* Call a crisis line, tell your parents or a friend, and report it to the police. Provide as much identifying information as you can:

physical descriptions, clothes, make and color of car, and any other details you can recall. More details will increase the chance for an arrest and conviction. If you suffer visible injuries in the assault, let the police, a doctor, or a friend take pictures of you. This type of physical evidence is invaluable at trial.

Coping with Date Rape and Acquaintance Rape by Andrea Parrott (Rosen Publishing Group, 1993). Preventive strategies on how to keep from being a victim, plus counsel and advice for those who have already become victims.

Everything You Need to Know About Date Rape by Frances Shuker-Haines (Rosen Publishing Group, 1992). What is date rape and whose fault is it? This book makes it clear that the victim is never at fault.

Past Forgiving by Gloria D. Miklowitz (Simon & Schuster, 1995). Fifteen-year-old Alexandra finds that her boyfriend, Cliff, demands all of her time, isolates her by his jealousy, and finally becomes physically abusive. A compelling novel, honest in its exploration of date rape and how love can go wrong.

Date Rape
http://www.ncpc.org/10yth3.htm
Information from the National Crime Prevention Council.

"Friends" Raping Friends: Could It Happen to You?
http://www.cs.utk.edu/~bartley/acquaint/acquaintRape.html#legal
An excellent resource, loaded with information. This site also includes a page on sexual assault information:
http://www.cs.utk.edu/~bartley/saInfoPage.html

RAINN (Rape, Abuse, and Incest National Network)
1-800-656-HOPE (1-800-656-4673)
Calls are routed to a rape crisis center in the caller's area code.

"Do I lose any rights if I'm pregnant?"

Not long ago, the answer to this question was a definite yes. In the 1970s, you could have been asked to drop out of school if you were an unwed pregnant minor, or you could have lost your job for taking maternity leave.

The law now allows you to continue your education if you're pregnant. You can't be discriminated against because you're pregnant or because you've had an abortion. Some school districts offer programs for pregnant teens, allowing them to obtain prenatal care and parenting classes, and to stay on track with academic schoolwork. Check to see if your district offers these opportunities.

You may also be able to obtain prenatal medical care, with or without your parents' consent. If your parents know about the pregnancy and are supportive, all the better. But if they don't know, or if they oppose it, you can still get the medical attention you and the baby need.*

In 1978, the Pregnancy Discrimination Act regarding employment was passed. The Act applies to you whether you're a teenager or an adult. It prohibits any discrimination based solely on your medical condition, resulting from an abortion or a pregnancy. If you're a full-time employee, you may take maternity leave (often without pay) and without fear of losing your job. This affects few teenagers because most aren't employed full-time. Depending on the circumstances, maternity leave may apply to teenage parents.

Justice Harry Blackmun said that the sex discrimination laws mean that "women as capable of doing their jobs as their male counterparts may not be forced to choose between having a child and having a job."—U.S. Supreme Court (1991), *Auto Workers v. Johnson Controls*

States may have their own laws on this subject, so check into your local rules or contact the Equal Employment Opportunity Office (EEOC).

The courts have gone one step further in eliminating discrimination against women in the workplace. The Supreme Court ruled in 1991 that employers can't exclude women of childbearing age from jobs that pose reproductive hazards, such as

---

* See pages 70–71.

industrial jobs. Gender-based discrimination, whether to protect the mother or her future children, is unlawful.

Campaign for Our Children
http://www.cfoc.org/
Lots of information about teen pregnancy. The site was designed for parents, but you can go here, too.

Teenage Pregnancy: Facts You Should Know
http://www.noah.cuny.edu/
Click on "Health Topics," then "Pregnancy," then "Teenage Pregnancy" for facts, resources, and more. A page on the award-winning "Ask NOAH" site, a joint project of the City University of New York, the New York Academy of Medicine, New York Metropolitan Reference and Research Library Agency, and the New York Public Library.

"What if I'm depressed or thinking about suicide?"

Everyone, regardless of age or circumstances, occasionally gets depressed or stressed out. Sadness, loneliness, or feelings of alienation from family and friends can hit anyone at any time.

Whatever is troubling you—no matter how big the problem—there's help available. Trained professionals can be reached at any time. Their services are confidential and nonjudgmental, and their purpose is to listen to you and offer suggestions to help you deal with what's going on in your life.

- 321 children between the ages of 5 and 14 committed suicide in 1993. Firearms were used in 187 of these deaths.
- 4,848 people between the ages of 15 and 24 committed suicide; 3,213 deaths were by firearms.

Source: *The State of America's Children Yearbook 1997,* Children's Defense Fund

You may have a friend or acquaintance who's feeling depressed or suicidal. Or perhaps he or she has already dealt with depression and could help you get through yours. Reach out and discuss the problem with someone you trust. If you're concerned about a friend, offer to help. If the situation is serious and you think your friend may hurt himself or herself, take action. Tell your parents, your friend's parents, or another responsible adult. Every state has laws regarding emergency mental health care. A brief placement in a hospital (twenty-four to seventy-two hours) for evaluation can start the healing process.

Whatever the issue—whether it's grades, relationship problems, or trouble with sports, a job, or drugs—help is nearby. Hotlines staffed with trained counselors can help you if you're suffering from depression or thinking about suicide.

Coping with Suicide by Judie Smith (Rosen Publishing Group, 1990). Ways for teens to deal with social pressures and problems.

Straight Talk About Anxiety and Depression by Michael Maloney and Rachel Kranz (Dell Publishing Co., 1993). Case studies, suggestions for coping, self-corrective behavior, and information for getting help.

The Power to Prevent Suicide: A Guide for Teens Helping Teens by Richard E. Nelson, Ph.D., and Judith C. Galas (Free Spirit Publishing, 1994). Understanding the causes of suicide, recognizing the signs, and reaching out to save a life.

American Association of Suicidology
4201 Connecticut Avenue NW, Suite 310
Washington, DC 20008
(202) 237-2280
http://www.cyberpsych.org
Information and referrals to support groups around the country.

Covenant House Nineline
1-800-999-9999
http://www.covenanthouse.org
Immediate crisis intervention, support, and referrals for runaways and abandoned youth, and those who are suicidal or in crisis. Help is available for children, teens, and adults.

Kids Help Phone
1-800-668-6868
http://kidshelp.sympatico.ca/
Canada's only toll-free national telephone counseling service for children
and youth ages 4–19.

National Youth Crisis Hotline
1-800-HIT-HOME (1-800-448-4663)
For children and teens struggling with problems of abuse, drugs, alcohol,
suicide, pregnancy, or sexual pressure. Operated by Youth Development
International *(http://www.ydi.org)*.

National Youth Crisis Hotline
1-800-442-HOPE (1-800-442-4673)
Operated by Children's Rights of America *(http://home/sprynet.com/
sprynet/CRA)*.

Self-Help Suicide Resources
http://www.cmhc.com/guide/suicidal.htm
An extensive collection of links compiled by Mental Health Net.

Suicide Awareness\Voices of Education (SA\VE)
http://www.save.org/
Frequently asked questions, danger signs, support for suicide survivors,
and more. Includes "What to Do If a Friend Has Depression: A Guide
for Students."

"When can I get a tattoo?"

You've probably had many conversations (or battles) with your
parents about your choice of hairstyle and color, earrings, and
style of dress. When it comes to body tattoos, piercing, and branding, your parents may have laid
down the law and said no way.

Legally, you must be eighteen
before getting a tattoo in most
states. Adults who violate existing
laws by tattooing a minor, or con-
senting to a tattoo in violation of
the law, are subject to penalties.
Branding and piercing body parts
are not yet covered by specific laws.

- In **Illinois,** tattoos may not be sold to anyone under 21.
- In **Arkansas, Pennsylvania,** and **Tennessee,** you must be 18 to get a tattoo.
- In **Rhode Island,** the tattooing age is also 18, but there is no age limit for the removal of tattoos.
- In **Arizona,** a 1996 law makes tattooing a minor without a parent or guardian present a felony, subject to a year in jail or up to a $150,000 penalty.

Once you become an adult, you can decide how to express and present yourself to others. Think it through before you act. Although laser treatment is available to remove the ink from a tattoo, the skin area is never 100 percent restored to its original state. Branding is even more difficult, if not impossible, to erase. Keep in mind that many employers, including national franchises, won't hire people who have visible markings. So before you tattoo or brand your fingers, hands, arms, or face, talk with some friends or adults who have had the experience. Contact the local job bank or a work placement counselor at school to find out what personal adornments are acceptable in your area.

"How old do I have to be to smoke?"

Tobacco—whether it takes the form of cigarettes, snuff, or smokeless (chewing) tobacco—is a subject of great concern to adults and teens. Several states are suing the tobacco industry to recover the rising costs of health care blamed on smoking. Tobacco companies are under pressure from the U.S. Food and Drug Administration (FDA) regarding the dangers of nicotine, its relationship to lung disease and other respiratory ailments, and its addictive properties.

In most states, you must be eighteen to smoke and buy tobacco products. A 1997 FDA ruling requires stores to ask for photo identification before selling cigarettes or chewing tobacco to

- An estimated 3,000 children begin smoking each day. 1,000 of them will die from a tobacco-related illness.
- Between 1991 and 1994, the percentage of eighth graders who smoke rose from 14 to 18%.
- Tobacco smoke contains at least 43 cancer-causing substances.
- One out of 5 high school seniors is a daily smoker.
- Smokers lose an average of 15 years of life.
- A 1997 survey of 16,000 teens ages 14–19 found that 26% (about 6 *million* teens) had tried cigars during the past year. Cigars contain as much as 40 times more tar and nicotine than cigarettes.

Sources: *Congressional Quarterly Researcher*, December, 1995; American Lung Association, New York, NY; *Centers for Disease Control and Prevention*

anyone who looks younger than twenty-seven. If you're caught violating the law, you and any adult involved can be prosecuted.

Even if you don't smoke or chew tobacco, breathing second-hand smoke has proven to be a health hazard. Consequently, many public buildings across the nation offer smoke-free environments or separate no-smoking sections. If you're caught smoking in a restricted area, you may be cited. If you're also underage, you'll receive a second citation.

Teenagers often think it's okay to light up because their parents and friends smoke. Some parents approve of their children smoking, and some even buy cigarettes for them. If you or a friend is in this situation, take a look at the statistics and decide for yourself if your health and future well-being are worth the risk.

American Cancer Society
1-800-227-2345
http://www.cancer.org
Call the toll-free number to be connected with the American Cancer Society office nearest you. Call or go online to get information about the Great American Smokeout® program, how to get help quitting smoking, and information about cancer treatment and prevention.

American Lung Association
1-800-LUNG-USA (1-800-586-4872)
http://www.lungusa.org
Contact the American Lung Association for information about lung health, smoking, air pollution, current national research reports, and much more.

Arizona Department of Health Services Tobacco Education and Prevention Program
1-800-404-9267
Request a copy of their "Smelly, Puking Habit" merchandise catalog, which offers T-shirts, hats, temporary tattoos, bandannas, posters, and other items for children, teens, and adults.

The BADvertising Institute
http://world.std.com/~batteryb/
The powerful images at this site will make you think twice about cigarette advertising and motivate you to quit smoking (or never start).

Kickbutt
http://www.kickbutt.org
Sponsored by Washington DOC (Doctors Ought to Care) to give young people accurate information about the physical and social effects of smoking. Includes how to quit, how to get involved in anti-tobacco activism, links to other sites, and much more.

Nicotine Anonymous
Nicotine Anonymous World Services
P.O. Box 591777
San Francisco, CA 94159-1777
(415) 750-0328
http://rampages.onramp.net/~nica/
Check the white pages of your local phone book for a group near you.

QuitNet
http://www.quitnet.org
Sponsored by the Tobacco Control Program at the Massachusetts Department of Public Health.

"When can I have a beer?"

You must be twenty-one in most states to buy or drink beer, wine, or any alcoholic beverage. If you break the law and are caught drinking, you may be fined and given community service hours to complete. The person who sells or gives you alcohol may also be prosecuted.

In **California,** you must be 21 before eating any candy, cake, cookie, or chewing gum that contains alcohol.

Even if you aren't legally *intoxicated* (your blood alcohol level is over your state's limit), you can still get into trouble for being *under the influence* of alcohol. This means that you aren't legally drunk, but your senses are affected. You may find yourself in dangerous situations and unable to make good choices when you have drugs or alcohol in your system. Poor decisions made under the influence may have a drastic impact on the rest of your life.

Between concerned family members, school, and community events, you've probably heard a lot about the dangers of alcohol, and the statistics speak for themselves. The medical facts are equally clear: alcohol damages your brain cells, inflames the stomach lining, kills liver cells, blocks memory, dulls your senses, and has been linked to birth defects in infants.

- Over 4 million teenagers in America have serious problems with alcohol.
- Approximately 30% of boys and 22% of girls classify themselves as drinkers by age 12.
- 28% of high school seniors are "binge drinkers," consuming 5 or more drinks at a time.
- Every year, over 3,000 teenagers are killed in drunk-driving crashes.
- Most teenage passengers are killed in accidents with teen drivers.
- Every 26 minutes, someone is killed in an alcohol-related accident.

Sources: National Safety Council; Students Against Driving Drunk (SADD)

Al-Anon and Alateen
1-800-344-2666
In Canada: 1-800-443-4525
http://www.al-anon.alateen.org/
Al-Anon is a worldwide organization that provides support to families and friends of alcoholics; Alateen is for younger family members who are affected by someone else's drinking. Request their free packet of teen materials.

Alcoholics Anonymous
AA World Services, Inc.
P.O. Box 459
Grand Central Station
New York, NY 10163
(212) 870-3400
http://www.alcoholics-anonymous.org/
Since its founding in 1935, AA has helped millions of men and women around the world to stop drinking.

American Council on Alcoholism Helpline
1-800-527-5344
Referrals to alcohol treatment programs nationwide and educational materials.

Mental Health Net
http://www.cmhc.com/selfhelp.htm
Tons of links to sites with self-help information on a wide variety of
health issues including alcohol and drug abuse.

Online AA Resources
http://www.recovery.org/aa/homepage.html
A comprehensive collection of information on AA with links to
related resources.

"What if I use or sell marijuana?"

Legislatures have passed laws against the use, sale, and possession
of marijuana. A few states (California and Arizona, for example)
have passed laws authorizing doctors to prescribe small amounts
of marijuana for personal medicinal use. These statewide sanc-
tions, however, are being challenged by national lawmakers.

- In 1995, 61,150 teens between ages 12 and 17 were admitted to hospital emergency rooms for drug episodes. Almost 11% of teens in this age group use drugs monthly.
- In 1996, 18% of eighth graders, 34% of tenth graders, and 36% of high school seniors reported using marijuana during the previous year.

Sources: *Juvenile Offenders and Victims: A National Report,* National Center for Juvenile Justice (1995), with 1996 *Update on Violence;* 1996 survey of 50,000 eighth grade and high school students by the University of Michigan and the National Institute on Drug Abuse

Violation of any drug law
will result in some form of legal
action. If a first offense involves a
small amount of marijuana, you
may be placed in a diversion program. This means you'll be required to attend drug information
classes and possibly participate in
random drug testing. After you
complete the classes, your case will
be closed, with no arrest or juvenile record. If you fail to complete the program, formal charges
may be filed. If you're convicted of a drug violation, penalties
include detention time, probation, and suspension or loss of your
driver's license.

Many teens claim that they turn to drugs to avoid pressure,
relieve stress, and help handle depression. But drugs, including
marijuana, are a health risk. (For example, marijuana contains up

to 400 chemicals that can pose major health hazards.) Believing that pot is the least dangerous of recreational drugs, more young people are using it—despite statistics showing that marijuana use often leads to experimentation with harder drugs.

A conviction on a marijuana charge goes on your record (through a local and national computer system that records arrests, convictions, and sentences) and can follow you throughout your life. Future job opportunities may be jeopardized because of teenage drug use or experimentation. A teacher in Illinois recently lost his job when a background check turned up a 1974 conviction for marijuana possession. A candidate for a U.S. Supreme Court appointment was disqualified after admitting he had used marijuana as a student.

There's help for anyone with a drug problem. A phone call to a local teen hotline, or any of the 12-Step programs in your community (Alcoholics Anonymous, Narcotics Anonymous, Cocaine Anonymous, etc.) is a first step toward recovery and a drug-free life. Check the white pages of your phone book for local listings.

If you have a problem with drugs or alcohol, get help! Medical care and counseling are available, and you may not need your parents' consent to participate. Early warning signs indicating a problem include:

- You have new friends who abuse alcohol/drugs.
- Your grades drop, you fail tests, or you miss a lot of classes.
- You withdraw from family and friends; you become isolated and lie about your drinking/drug use.
- You experience mood swings, depression, and a loss of interest in your usual activities.

Legislatures have lowered the minimum age for obtaining help for alcohol and other drug use to encourage teenagers to take action. If you're afraid to go to your parents for help, ask your school nurse or counselor, or call a confidential hotline.

Drugs and Where to Turn by Bea O'Donnell Rawls and Gwen Johnson (Rosen Publishing Group, 1993). Teens who use drugs can often find themselves "in too deep." Afraid to tell their parents, teachers, or other authority figures, they need sources of information and guidance. This book contains suggestions, hotlines, and organizations that will provide vital information for troubled teens.

Taking Charge of My Mind & Body: A Girls' Guide to Outsmarting Alcohol, Drug, Smoking, and Eating Problems by Gladys Folkers, M.A., and Jeanne Engelmann (Free Spirit Publishing, 1997). Facts about alcohol, drugs, smoking, and eating problems, myths and reality checks, warning signs, and strategies for building resistance skills.

Center for Substance Abuse Treatment (CSAT)
1-800-662-HELP (1-800-662-4357)
For counseling and referrals in emergencies.

Cocaine Anonymous
1-800-347-8998
http://www.ca.org/
Information about the national organization and local groups. Not a hotline.

Cocaine Hotline
1-800-COCAINE (1-800-262-2463)
Answers emergency questions about cocaine and other drug use; provides counseling and referrals.

D.A.R.E. (Drug Abuse Resistance Education)
1-800-223-3273
http://www.dare-america.com/
Information on D.A.R.E.'s anti-drug, anti-violence message for kids, parents, educators, and D.A.R.E. officers.

"Don't Lose a Friend to Drugs" Factsheet
http://www.ncpc.org/10yth2.htm
From the National Crime Prevention Council.

Drug Abuse Information and Treatment Referral Line
1-800-821-4357
For drug-related information, referrals to local treatment programs, and support.

Marijuana Anonymous
1-800-766-6779
http://www.marijuana-anonymous.org/
Information and local referrals.

Narcotics Anonymous
(818) 773-9999
http://www.wsoinc.com/

National Clearinghouse for Alcohol and Drug Information (NCADI)
1-800-SAY-NO-TO (1-800-729-6686)
http://www.health.org
An organization of the federal government providing free information on substance abuse.

National Drug and Alcohol Treatment and Referral Hotline
1-800-662-4357
A hotline for information, referrals, and crisis counseling, sponsored by the U.S. Department of Health and Human Services.

Web of Addictions
http://www.well.com/user/woa/
This award-winning sight is packed with factual information, links, and resources on alcohol and drug abuse.

"Is it against the law to sniff glue or paint?"

When fourteen-year-old Randy tried to get high with his friends, he made the headlines: "Teen Dies After Sniffing ScotchGuard." He lost consciousness while sniffing the fumes of a common household spray. Inhalant abuse causes approximately 1,000 deaths in the U.S. each year.

Young children and teenagers are experimenting more and more with inhaling everything from glue to spray paint, gasoline, lighter fluid, paint thinner, and air fresheners. Other household products that contain breathable vapors include shoe polish, typewriter correction fluid, hair spray, and bug killers. The vapors or fumes from these products starve the body of oxygen, which causes damage to the brain and nervous system and sometimes

- A 1994 survey of 12- to 17-year-olds revealed that 2% of them used inhalants, which followed alcohol and marijuana in popularity.
- 17% of high school seniors have used inhalants.

Sources: *Juvenile Offenders and Victims: A National Report,* National Center for Juvenile Justice (1995), with 1996 *Update on Violence; Statistical Abstract of the United States 1996,* U.S. Department of Commerce

leads to death. Brain cells killed by sniffing substances can't be replaced, and frequent users often undergo personality changes.

States have laws against inhaling toxic vapors. If you're caught sniffing, you may be locked up until counseling begins. Passing laws against the use or purchase of these products by minors is helping, but it hasn't solved the problem.

Think About It, Talk About It

1. Summer is near, and it's warmer out. One of your friends has stopped hanging out with you. You and everyone else dress in shorts and T-shirts, but he's always in jeans and long-sleeved shirts.

You suspect that he's being abused. What should you do?

2. Your brother is nineteen and pretty much does what he wants. Although you have to be twenty-one to buy alcohol in your state, anyone can easily get it. He drinks, smokes, and uses marijuana. He says he's an adult, and if he's old enough to go to war and die, he's entitled to do as he pleases.

In a way, this makes sense, doesn't it? Why or why not?

3. What would you say to a friend who told you he or she would like to quit smoking but can't?

4. What can you do to help in the fight against teen smoking?

5. You see a page in your best friend's journal and discover a poem about depression and wanting to commit suicide. What should you do?

Chapter 5

Growing Up

"You grow up the day you have your
first real laugh—at yourself."
Ethel Barrymore, American actress

As you approach eighteen, you'll start to think more about your future. Whether that includes continuing your education, getting a job, traveling, interning, or a combination of all four, you'll need to do some planning. You'll also benefit from an awareness of your rights and obligations.

Adulthood means taking on new responsibilities. Your relationships with others, whether personal, business, or social, go through many changes. Once you legally become an adult, you stand on your own. You own the consequences of your successes and failures.

This chapter discusses a variety of subjects related to growing up. You'll learn about traffic laws, the right to change your name, the meaning of emancipation, getting your own place (and the ups and downs of being independent of your parents), and, finally, your rights and duties regarding the government in terms of voting, military service, and running for public office. If possible, talk

If you're wondering what other teens are doing, here are some recent statistics:

- In 1996, 6.4 million teens ages 16–19 were employed.
- 1.5 million teens were enrolled in college (62% of the 1994 high school graduates).
- High school seniors in 1992 did the following types of work:

Food service	24%
Grocery store	14%
Sales	11%
Office/clerical	7%
Baby-sitting	4%

Sources: *Digest of Education Statistics 1996*, U.S. Department of Education; *Monthly Labor Review*, U.S. Department of Labor

about these subjects with your parents and friends. An important part of growing up is knowing when to ask questions and seek help from others.

"When will I be an adult?"

Anyone under the age of eighteen is referred to as a *minor,* a *child,* a *juvenile,* or an *adolescent.* The term used depends on the situation. Once you turn eighteen, you're legally an *adult,* with all of the rights and obligations of adulthood.

Turning eighteen, or the "age of majority" (in most states), entitles you to complete independence—in most situations. You can enjoy the freedom to move away from home, buy a car, work full-time or travel, marry, vote, and join the armed services. In other words, major decisions about your life are yours to make.

> "Constitutional rights do not mature and come into being magically only when one attains the state-defined age of majority. Minors, as well as adults, are protected by the Constitution and possess constitutional rights." —U.S. Supreme Court (1976), *Planned Parenthood v. Danforth*

This is not to say that your parents are automatically excluded, especially if they continue to support you. There's nothing magical about turning eighteen. The legal rights you now enjoy are balanced with certain obligations and responsibilities.

"What does emancipation mean?"

At some point before your eighteenth birthday, you'll probably think about being free—that's *emancipation.* But what does it mean exactly? What are the legal consequences of being "free" from your parents? Are there any drawbacks to emancipation before you turn eighteen?

An emancipated person is legally free from his or her parents or legal guardian. This means that your parents are no longer responsible for you or your actions, and you no longer have the right to be taken care of by them. The legal consequences of emancipation are the same as though you were eighteen.

A teenager becomes emancipated in one of two ways: either by a court order (if your state has an emancipation law) or by certain other circumstances. Not all states have emancipation laws. Some states with emancipation laws include Alabama, Arkansas, California, Illinois, Indiana, Kansas, Louisiana, Michigan, Mississippi, North Carolina, Oklahoma, and Tennessee. If your state has an emancipation law, take a look at the law and follow its requirements, and the court will either grant or deny your request for emancipation. For example, you may have to show the court that you have a job, live on your own, and pay your bills, and that your parents don't claim you as a dependent on their taxes. The court may then declare you a legally free teenager. Your lifestyle is taken into consideration in determining whether you're emancipated or not.

> "Unemancipated minors . . . are subject . . . as to their physical freedom, to the control of their parents or guardians . . . they lack the right to come and go at will."—U.S. Supreme Court (1995), *Vernonia School Dist. v. Acton*

If your state doesn't have an emancipation law, you still may become legally free from your parents before you're eighteen. If you join the armed services or get married, you're considered independent of your parents. Most states acknowledge your independence if either of these events occur before you reach the age of majority.

Teenagers who run away or are kicked out of their homes aren't legally emancipated. Their parents may still be held responsible for their actions and will continue to have authority over them.*

Responsibility shifts from your parents or guardians to you once you're emancipated. You still may not have all the rights and privileges of adulthood (being able to vote, enter into contracts, buy property, etc.), but the experience of living independently while you're sixteen or seventeen will be a learning experience in preparation for your complete independence.

---

* See Chapter 7, pages 140–141.

If you're emancipated and face a problem or situation that's new to you, get some advice. Talk with someone you trust before you act or make a decision.

"Can I change my name?"

Once in a while, you might think about changing your name. (Some parents have saddled their kids with terrible, embarrassing names.) For any number of reasons, a different first, middle, or last name might seem like a good idea.

Before state laws were passed regarding name changes, any person, including a minor, could change his or her name simply by using the new name. Today, in most states you must be eighteen to obtain a legal name change. Other states allow underage persons to apply if parental consent is given. You can apply to your local court—it may be the family, juvenile, or probate court, depending on your state. The court will consider your reasons for seeking a name change. If you're doing it to avoid paying bills, for example, your request will be denied. As long as you're not breaking the law or attempting to hide something, the name change will be allowed. The court will issue an order indicating the new name, with a copy to you.

Name changing isn't a right enjoyed in all countries.

- In **Denmark,** parents can give their children only government-approved names.
- In **France,** if a judge finds that a child's first name is contrary to the child's best interests, the court may give the child a new name.

Other opportunities to change your name occur when you get married or adopted. Marriage often results in a change of last name for the bride. However, she may choose to keep her maiden name, or use both names—her husband's with her maiden name, sometimes in a hyphenated form. Your marriage license and/or certificate will reflect any name changes.

When you're adopted, you have the opportunity to obtain an entirely new name—first, middle, and last. Your adoptive parents will decide on the names for you, but if you're a teenager, you'll most likely have a say. At the final adoption hearing, the judge will go over your new name with you. That's the time to speak up. If you don't agree or you want something different, tell your parents and the court. Once the adoption is granted, a new birth certificate will be issued stating your new legal name.

Recent court cases show that there are a number of other circumstances for changing your name. A change of last name may be appropriate where a parent's misconduct (criminal acts, for example) places a child at risk. A child may be allowed to add his or her stepparent's last name to his or her name, to reinforce a new identity and relieve anxieties. Sometimes the courts have ruled *against* name changes for teens. In a 1992 Pennsylvania case, a mother's attempt to change her son's last name following a bitter divorce was denied. The name change wasn't considered to be in the boy's best interests.

> In 1993, a New Jersey court allowed a boy named Redfreddy to change his name to Andrew. Redfreddy's mother was mentally ill and lived in a psychiatric hospital. His father was unknown. The court called his name "plainly ridiculous" and wished to spare the child from future difficulties.

If you legally change your name while you're a teenager, either you and/or your parents need to notify all parties who have you officially listed under your old name. Provide a copy of the court order changing your name to your school, doctor, bank, insurance company, and employer. You'll also need to get a new driver's license and new credit cards if they were issued in your previous name. Changing your name carries with it an obligation to avoid confusion by letting the appropriate people know your new name.

"When can I get my own apartment?"

If you're under eighteen, most landlords won't rent to you without a parent or guardian co-signing the lease. This may be age discrimination, but it isn't illegal. Owners and landlords require a legally responsible adult to be on the lease or rental agreement.

Once you've moved in, you're required to pay the monthly rent and whatever additional expenses are spelled out in your agreement. This may include the first and last month's rent, utilities (gas, electric, water), the phone bill, and a security or damage deposit. If your name is on the lease, you're legally responsible for the apartment and for paying the expenses for the entire term of the lease.

You'll be given firm dates for paying your rent and the terms for any damage to the property. If you leave the place in the same condition as when you moved in, your security deposit will be refunded. Read your lease agreement carefully before signing it, and don't forget to keep a copy for yourself. Go over it with your parents and read the fine print.

If you have valuable personal property in your new place, consider buying renter's insurance. It may seem like an unnecessary expense, but if someone breaks in and takes your clothes, stereo, and sporting equipment, you'll be left empty-handed unless you have insurance. If you're covered, you'll be able to replace what's been stolen.

"Can I have a gun?"

As a general rule, firearms may not be sold to minors. Your parents must agree before you can have a gun, ammunition, or any toy gun that shoots a dangerous or explosive substance. BB guns, air rifles, and pistols may be considered weapons and should be used only under adult supervision.

Check with your local sporting goods store or game and fish department about the laws in your area. If you're given the chance to take a firearms safety course, sign up—even if you think you're familiar with weapons. If a friend wants to go hunting or target practicing with you, ask him or her to also take the class.

- 16 persons under age 19 are killed every day by firearms.
- 135,000 children bring a gun to school every day.
- Between 1980 and 1994, 25 Americans died from BB or pellet gun injuries.

Sources: *Accident Facts 1996*, National Safety Council; *The State of America's Children Yearbook 1997*, Children's Defense Fund

You're probably aware of the rules about weapons (like guns and knives) at school. Even if you're asked to hold a weapon for a friend or store it in your locker, don't! Under the law, school authorities may search your locker, and if you possess a weapon, even for a brief time, you're at fault.

In May, 1996, a sixteen-year-old junior in Wichita, Kansas, was expelled for his senior year for having a paintball gun in his car at school. Jeremy was a football player, a yell leader, and a member of the National Honor Society, with a 3.6 grade point average. He had participated in a paintball tournament the night before, and afterward threw the gun in the back of his car. Jeremy's school, like many others, has a "zero tolerance" policy on weapons at school—whether real or realistic-looking replicas. With guns (and even gun look-alikes), the bottom line is to know the laws in your state, community, and school—and follow them.

- Anyone in **Alabama** who sells, lends, or gives you a Bowie knife has broken the law.
- In **Maryland,** children's toys depicting torture or torture instruments are restricted.
- It's now illegal to sell box cutters, an increasingly popular weapon, to minors in **New York City.**
- In **Virginia,** cap guns are okay, but any firearm that discharges blanks or ball charges are restricted.

FYI

Gun Control: Current Controversies, edited by Tamara L. Roleff (Greenhaven Press, 1997). Various authors discuss the benefits and problems posed by gun control and gun ownership.

Think About Guns in America by Helen Strahinich (Walker, 1992). Discusses types of guns, the history of guns, gun control laws, and specifics of actual cases of gun violence.

"When can I vote?"

It wasn't that long ago that the right to vote in this country became universal. In your parents' lifetime, millions of Americans were prevented from voting. Some states had what was called a *poll* or *head tax*. Adults who wished to vote were required to pay a tax, so those who couldn't afford the tax were unable to vote. Literacy tests were also required, and those who couldn't pass the test were denied the right to vote. Between 1964 and 1966, both the poll tax and voter registration tests were eliminated as unconstitutional. The Civil Rights Act of 1965 and the U.S. Supreme Court opened the door to full voter participation by all U.S. citizens.

In 1971, the 26th Amendment to the U.S. Constitution was passed. It granted all citizens eighteen years of age or older the right to vote. This applies to you and is without any restrictions. You merely need to register where you live and exercise your right by voting at every opportunity. This is one of the greatest rights Americans have. It allows us to choose our leaders and speak our minds on the issues before us—but not just on a national level. Don't think of local, city, town, or county elections as insignificant or unimportant. Decisions made by these elected officials affect your life, too.

Information about how and where to register to vote is available at your local elections office or post office. A registrar might also be available to come to your home. California has "high school voter weeks," when you may register to vote at school during the last two weeks of September and April. Take advantage of this kind of registration opportunity, then vote when elections are held. If you know in advance that you'll be on vacation or away from your voting precinct on election day, arrange for an absentee ballot. Your local elections office or registrar will help you.

FYI

Kids Voting USA is a nonprofit, nonpartisan organization that enables children and teens to visit official polling sites on election days and cast their own ballots on the same issues and candidates the adults are voting for. Speakers are available to come to your school and address civics and social studies classes. To date, 41 states and the District of Columbia are members of the Kids Voting USA network. For more information (and to find out if your state is a member), contact:

Kids Voting USA
398 South Mill Ave., Suite 304
Tempe, AZ 85281
(602) 921-3727
http://www.kidsvotingusa.org/Home.html

"Can I run for public office?"

Once you're eighteen, you may be eligible for various public offices. All three branches of government have positions filled by elected officials. The *executive* branch includes state governors and the U.S. president and the vice-president; the *legislative* branch includes state representatives and senators, as well as Congress; and the *judicial* branch consists of elected judges. City, county, and town offices are also staffed by elected officials.

Due to variations from state to state, you'll have to check out the exact requirements of the office you're interested in. Age and residency requirements may affect your decision to run. For example, to run for president of the United States, you must be thirty-five years old, a natural-born U.S. citizen, and a U.S. resident for at least fourteen years.

You might want to start out by exploring opportunities on the local level of government, and you can get involved while still in school. Join a student club or local political organization (such as the Young Democrats, Young Republicans, or groups affiliated with the Reform Party, Green Party, or other political organizations). Volunteer to help with a local campaign—stuffing envelopes, working a phone bank, or distributing literature. Learning all aspects of a campaign will come in handy down the road.

"Will I get drafted?"

Throughout U.S. history, young men have been called for military service. From colonial times through the Vietnam War, eligible males over eighteen have been drafted. In 1973, the government ended the draft, replacing it with a "stand-by draft" for men and voluntary service for men and women. All males, within thirty days of their eighteenth birthday and continuing up to age twenty-six, are required to register with the Selective Service System. This rule doesn't apply to women. Registration provides the government with a list of men to call up for service in the event of a national emergency. Failure to register is a crime with a penalty of five years in prison or a $250,000 fine.

Men and women may join the army, navy, air force, marines, national guard, or coast guard. If you're interested, contact your local recruiter. He or she will give you complete information about enlisting, including benefits, length of service, and education and travel opportunities. If you're thinking of a career in the military as an officer, contact the Naval Academy in Annapolis, Maryland; the Air Force Academy in Colorado Springs, Colorado; or the Army's U.S. Military Academy in West Point, New York, for information.

You may not be eligible to join the armed services because of your age. Not all branches will take you if you're under eighteen, unless you have your parents' consent or you're emancipated. You may also need your high school diploma or GED certificate to enlist. Some branches won't take you if you're on probation or parole, or if you have a juvenile record. You may need to ask the court to destroy your record, which will clear the way for your enlistment.* These are all questions to discuss with your recruiter.

If, by reason of religious training or belief, you object to military training and service, you may be excused from active duty. A *conscientious objector* is protected by the U.S. Constitution and the Bill

---

* See Chapter 8, pages 170–171.

of Rights. You must still register with the Selective Service System, but you may be permitted to serve through noncombat civilian service. Discuss this with your parents before deciding what to do.

Selective Service System
P.O. Box 94732
Palatine, IL 60094-4732
(847) 688-2576

U.S. Air Force Academy
Colorado Springs, CO 80840-5151
(719) 333-1818
http://www.af.mil/

U.S. Military Academy
West Point, NY 10996-5000
(914) 938-4011
http://www.usma.edu

U.S. Naval Academy
Annapolis, MD 21402
(410) 293-1000
http://www.nadn.navy.mil

"When can I get married?"

If you're eighteen, you may marry without anyone's permission. If you're not eighteen, you'll need permission from your parents or guardians and/or the court. States have different requirements about underage persons obtaining a marriage license. Some states also require a blood test and counseling before issuing a license.

There may also be restrictions on who you can marry. Marrying certain relatives (first or second cousins, for example) is against the law, but exactly which other relatives varies among the states. Under current law, gay and lesbian couples may not marry.

Legislation and lawsuits debating this issue are underway in a number of states. In a few cities, gay and lesbian couples may register as domestic partners.

If you get married as a teenager, you're considered emancipated. You're legally free from your parents, and they're no longer responsible for you. Likewise, you're no longer under their authority. Some states, noting the high incidence of divorce, reinstate the parent-child relationship if a married teenager gets divorced and returns home.

The latest figures regarding marriage and divorce show that:
- 2.3 million marriages and 1.1 million divorces took place in 1994.
- 11% of the marriages were with women under 20; 4.3% were with men under 20.
- The average length of marriages, as of 1990, was 7 years.

Source: *Statistical Abstract of the United States 1996*, U.S. Department of Commerce

As an emancipated, married teen, you should be able to obtain medical care on your own. And you may find it easier to enter into certain contracts and business relationships. Renting an apartment and obtaining credit may be easier, but alcohol remains off-limits until you turn twenty-one.

"What rights do teen parents have?"

The law doesn't distinguish between teen and adult parents. A parent's duty to nourish, love, and support a child doesn't start at age eighteen—it begins at parenthood, no matter how old you are. Some states require the parents of a teen mother or father to help out financially with their grandchild until the parents are adults.

As a parent, all decisions regarding your child's care are yours. This includes clothing, diet, child care, and medical care and treatment. Make sure your child's shots are current, and take your child to a doctor when needed. If your child is neglected or abused, the state may remove him or her from your custody.*

If you're a single parent or you get divorced while you're a teenager, you have the right to seek custody of your child. If

---

* See Chapter 4, pages 74–75.

you're unable to reach an agreement with the child's other parent, a court will decide where the child will live, along with visitation and support issues. Most teen parents in this situation find it best for the child to remain with the mother, with liberal visitation rights given to the father. Shared or joint custody is rare with young parents because of job, school, and transportation restrictions. The best interests of the child are considered first and foremost in deciding these issues.

Several programs to assist teen fathers have sprung up around the country. To promote responsible fatherhood or visitation and support by noncustodial fathers, communities are directing attention to young fathers.

You also have the right to place your child with the state or an agency if you're unable or unwilling to continue parenting. If you find the stress and pressure of being a parent overwhelming, ask for help. You can voluntarily place your child in a foster home or nursery while you work on

- The Responsible Teen Parent Program in **Tennessee** refers fathers for job training.
- The Teen Alternative Parenting Program (TAPP) in **Indiana** (among other states) allows teen fathers to earn credits against their child support obligation by participating in regular visits, parenting classes, schooling, and job training. In some communities, TAPP is referred to as "On Track."
- The Teen Father Program in **Cleveland, Ohio,** is aimed at inner-city neighborhoods. Rather than meeting in an office or clinic, services are provided within the teen's home.

solving whatever problems you have. This doesn't mean you're giving up your child permanently. It's only a temporary placement while you get help.

Other assistance available to teen parents includes food stamps, financial aid from the government through Aid to Families with Dependent Children (AFDC), and the Women, Infants and Children program (WIC) for low-income pregnant mothers. New welfare reform measures will limit benefits to eligible parents. Young parents will be affected by the five-year lifetime limit on all benefits, leaving the seventeen-year-old mother, for example, without AFDC, food stamps, or WIC after she's twenty-two. Check with your local benefits office for specific information.

If you decide not to keep your child, you have the right to sign a *consent for adoption*. Each state has specific requirements regarding adoption consents. Check first with an adoption agency, counselor, or lawyer. Be very careful about what you sign. Make sure you're fully informed about the law and the consequences of signing adoption papers. In many states, once you sign, it's final. Unless you can prove fraud or undue influence when you signed the consent, you can't get your child back if you later change your mind.

Coping with Teenage Motherhood by Carolyn Simpson (Rosen Publishing Group, 1992). A positive, nonjudgmental guide for married or single teens in all stages and situations of childbearing, with sound information on what to expect physically and emotionally.

Teenage Fathers by Karen Gravelle and Leslie Peterson (Julian Messner, 1992). Explores various aspects of teenage fatherhood through the experiences of thirteen teenage fathers.

Bureau for At-Risk Youth
1-800-99-YOUTH (1-800-999-6884)
http://www.at-risk.com/
Help and advice for raising happy, healthy children.

Many community and religious organizations conduct parenting classes. Call Child Protective Services (CPS), an adoption agency, or a family counseling center for a specific referral.

"Do traffic laws apply to me?"

Many of the rules of the motor vehicle code apply to you, whether or not you have a learner's permit or a driver's license. Traffic laws exist for the benefit and safety of passengers and pedestrians, as well as the person behind the wheel.

For example, crossing the street anywhere but in a crosswalk or at a traffic signal (jaywalking) may be against the law in your state. The same is true for hitch-hiking and walking in the street off the sidewalk. You may be fined or given community service hours for each offense.

Your local traffic laws may also apply to bicycle riders. One law, for example, requires that you ride only on a regular and permanent seat, and only one person per seat. In some places, if a passenger is under four years of age or under forty pounds, he or she must wear a helmet. Wearing a personal stereo headset while bicycling may also be illegal. Holding onto a moving car while on a bike, inline skates, or skateboard is both dangerous and against the law.

Bike paths are to be used wherever they're available, and all riders should keep at least one hand on the handlebars at all times. Bike riding while under the influence of drugs or alcohol is illegal.

If you're riding at night, your bike should have a white or yellow reflector on the front and a red one on the back. Your town may also have special laws regarding the use of skateboards, inline skates, and go-peds.

If you break a traffic law, the judge may do one or more of the following:

- talk to you about the incident and the driving laws of your state
- ask the county or district attorney to take a look at the case and consider filing a charge against you
- take your license or permit away for a period of time or restrict your driving

> - In 1995, 351 persons under age 24 died from bicycle-car accidents.
> - There were 25,486 reported injuries from skateboarding in 1995, and 99,500 inline skating injuries serious enough to send skaters to the emergency room.
>
> **Source:** *Accident Facts 1996,* National Safety Council

> - You're required to wear a helmet and elbow and knee pads if you're skateboarding at a skateboard park in **California.** Motorized skateboarding is prohibited on sidewalks, roadways, bike paths, or trails. In some areas, drivers of motorized scooters are being cited for no headlights, brake lights, or license plates.
> - In **Vermont,** go-cart races are regulated, and drivers must be 16. Anyone under the influence of drugs or alcohol is turned away.

- order you to go to traffic school
- order you to pay a fine, which could be hundreds of dollars
- order you to be supervised by a probation officer for a period of time
- require you to fix your car so it meets the minimum requirements of the law
- order you to complete a number of community service hours.

The bottom line is to know what the laws are where you live, follow them, and use common sense and caution regarding all traffic situations.

"When can I drive the family car?"

In many states, you may obtain a learner's permit before getting your license. It's a violation if you drive without either a permit or license. States differ on the exact age requirements for permits and licenses. If you're a student and taking a driving course, you may apply for a student license and, once you're fifteen or sixteen, apply for a driver's license. Your mom or dad must sign the application with you, and they're responsible for your driving. If you're in foster care, you may ask your guardian or foster parent to sign.

Under special circumstances, your state may issue a junior permit so you can drive at a younger age. This is possible in some rural areas where transportation to and from school is limited. There are also exceptions for driving farm equipment; some states don't require you to be licensed. Check first before you operate any vehicle. When driving with a learner's permit, you must be accompanied by a responsible licensed driver.

If you hit someone or damage someone's property while driving, you and your parents are responsible for the hospital or repair bills. It's illegal and extremely dangerous to drive under the influence of alcohol or drugs. You must be twenty-one to drink in the first place, so you're committing two violations if you're under twenty-one *and* drinking and driving. If you've been drinking or using drugs, make arrangements to ride with a sober designated driver.

Once you're issued a driver's license, you automatically agree to take a test given by a police officer if you're suspected of drinking and driving. This test measures the amount of alcohol in your body, and it may be used as evidence in court. If the amount is over the legal limit, you're considered either under the influence of alcohol or intoxicated. You may be required to attend counseling or an alcohol education program.

- In **Louisiana,** a 14-year-old can get a school instruction permit to drive.
- In **Mississippi,** you don't need a license to drive road machinery or a farm tractor.
- A 15-year-old in **South Carolina** can't drive at night (between 6:00 P.M. and 6:00 A.M.) without a parent, guardian, or licensed 21-year-old riding along.

Some states offer a Youthful Drunk Driver Visitation Program, in which you visit an alcohol recovery center, a hospital emergency room to witness persons injured in drunk-driving accidents, or the county morgue to view victims of drunk drivers. You may also be placed on probation or have your license suspended for a period of time.

FYI

Drugs and Driving by Janet Grosshandler (Rosen Publishing Group, 1992). Life-saving advice to teens struggling with peer pressure and friends or family under the influence.

Teen New Drivers' Homepage
http://www.ai.net/~ryanb/
Tips, information, commonsense advice, and links for new drivers from a new driver.

"Do I have to wear a helmet when I ride a motorcycle?"

Would you skydive for the first time without receiving landing instructions? How about suiting up without pads for Friday night's football game against your rival school? It's common sense to wear a helmet when riding a motorcycle, although some states don't require you to wear one. In other states, however, anyone under eighteen is required to wear a helmet while on a motorcycle (whether driving or riding as a passenger). Check the laws in your state, and remember that wearing a motorcycle helmet could save your life.

• The chances of being in an accident on a motorcycle are 17 times greater than in a car, truck, or bus.

• In 1995, 2,400 motorcycle riders were killed, and approximately 56,000 were injured.

• Helmets saved the lives of 527 motorcyclists in 1994.

Source: *Accident Facts 1996*, National Safety Council

The same goes for riding bicycles. A dozen states and about fifteen communities currently require children to wear a helmet while biking. Education about bike safety, less expensive helmets, and legislation have helped to increase the number of children in the U.S. who wear bike helmets.

"What is joyriding?"

Joyriding is defined as borrowing someone's car, bicycle, boat, or motorcycle without permission, with the intention of just using it for a while. Although joyriding isn't considered theft, it's still illegal because the owner's permission wasn't given.

It doesn't make any difference how long you keep the vehicle before returning it, or if you were only a passenger. If you know that the vehicle has been taken without the owner's consent, and you ride around in it, you're still held responsible. You don't have to be the one who took it or drove it to be considered accountable. Any damage to the vehicle may also become all or part of your responsibility. The exact circumstances surrounding the incident will be considered in determining the consequences.

In most jurisdictions, joyriding is a misdemeanor. Penalties for first-time offenders include diversion (counseling and community service hours) or a short probation period (possibly six months). If you're caught again, additional probation or intensive probation is possible, as well as house arrest or detention. If you have a driver's license or permit, it may be taken away.

In a 1997 decision, the U.S. Supreme Court ruled that police officers may order passengers out of the cars they stop for routine traffic violations. The police don't have to suspect that they are in danger, or that the passengers in the car have committed a crime.

"What are the penalties for drinking and driving?"

Automobile accidents are the top killer of teens in the U.S., with 42 percent of the accidents due to alcohol. There are different tickets involved in an alcohol-related incident: one for *driving while intoxicated* (DWI) and another for *driving under the influence* (DUI). If you're stopped by the police, you may be asked to take a test to check the alcohol level in your blood. Remember that when you apply for a driver's license, you automatically agree to being tested upon request for your blood-alcohol level. If you refuse to take the test, your license may be suspended.

- 20% of young adults ages 18–30 occasionally drive drunk. On any given night, 40% of young adults drink enough to impair their mental and physical performance.
- 120,000 juveniles were arrested in 1994 for liquor law violations. Over 18,000 were arrested for being drunk.

Source: *Juvenile Offenders and Victims: A National Report*, National Center for Juvenile Justice (1995), with 1996 *Update on Violence*

The test given may be a field sobriety test involving physical exercises at the scene to determine your physical state—touching your nose, picking up a coin while standing on one foot, etc. The officer may also check your eyes for dilation or rapid movements.

Or you may be asked to take a breath or blood test. Either of these gives a reading indicating your level of sobriety.

If your blood-alcohol level is *under* the state's legal limit (for example, .08 or .10), you may be cited for driving under the influence. If your level is *at* or *over* the limit, you'll receive a ticket for driving while intoxicated.

The penalties for either offense are serious and are becoming even more strict across the nation. Loss of your driver's license for a period of time is common practice, while substantial jail time is imposed for second and subsequent offenses. You'll also notice a significant increase in your car insurance. A DUI or DWI stays on your record for years. Your insurance agent can give you the specifics under your state's laws.

Related offenses cover such incidents as having an open beer or wine bottle in your car, soliciting someone to buy alcohol for you, and buying alcohol for a minor. All carry stiff penalties with far-reaching effects.

MADD (Mothers Against Drunk Driving)
1-800-438-MADD (1-800-438-6233)
http://www.madd.org/
For information on drunk driving for teens ("the 411 for the Under 21 crowd"), go to:
http://www.madd.org/under21/default.html

SADD (Students Against Driving Drunk)
National SADD
P.O. Box 800
Marlborough, MA 01752
(508) 481-3568
http://www.dot.gov/affairs/sadd.htm
Consider signing the SADD "Contract for Life" with your parents. You'll find a copy of the contract on page 115. To get your own signable copy, contact SADD.

CONTRACT FOR LIFE

A FOUNDATION FOR TRUST & CARING

By agreeing to this contract, we recognize that SADD encourages all young people to adopt a **substance-free** life style. We view this contract as a means of opening the lines of communication about drinking, drug use and traffic safety to ensure the safety of all parties concerned. We understand that this contract does not serve as permission to drink, but rather, a promise to be safe.

Young Adult

I acknowledge that the legal drinking age is 21 and have discussed with you and realize both the legal and physical risks of substance use, as well as driving under the influence. I agree to contact you if I ever find myself in a position where anyone's substance use impairs the possibility of my arriving home safely. I further pledge to maintain safe driving practices at all times, including wearing my safety belt every trip and encouraging others to do the same.

_____
Signature

Parent or Guardian:

Upon discussing this contract with you, I agree to arrange for your safe transportation home, regardless of time or circumstances. I further vow to remain calm when dealing with your situation and discuss it with you at a time when we are _both_ able to converse calmly about the matter.

I agree to seek safe, sober transportation home if I am ever in a situation where I have had too much to drink or a friend who is driving me has had too much to drink. Recognizing that safety belt usage is a vital defense against death and injury on the highway, I promise to wear my safety belt at all times and encourage others to do the same.

_____
Signature

_____
Date

Distributed by S.A.D.D. "Students Against Driving Drunk"

SADD and all the SADD logos are registered with the United States Patent and Trademark Office and other jurisdictions. All rights reserved by SADD, Inc., a Massachusetts non-profit corporation. Copying of this material is prohibited unless written permission received.

"Do water safety rules apply to teens?"

All people involved in recreational sports are required to follow water safety laws—whether posted or not. Violations result in heavy fines or loss of water privileges.

• All recreational boats are required to carry one wearable life jacket for each passenger. It should be bright orange or yellow, and be able to keep the person's head and mouth clear of the water.
• It's against the law in **Kansas** to be reckless while surfing, or to surf under the influence of drugs or alcohol.

Whether you go boating, waterskiing, or surfing, you should be aware of the safety rules. Speed signs, seating rules, and life jacket regulations apply to teenagers and adults alike. Making sure that your boat has the proper safety equipment, that you water ski without endangering swimmers or other skiers, or that you surf in marked areas is your responsibility. If your state permits teenagers to drive speedboats, it's your job to see that your passengers follow all water safety rules. During waterskiing, you need to designate someone to hold and properly use the flag to signal other boaters when the skier is down.

Generally, children under twelve aren't permitted to operate a boat or any type of watercraft, unless it's an emergency. There may be an exception for boats with low horsepower, or if an adult is present. If you're caught under the influence of alcohol or drugs while boating, you could get fined, or you might have to spend a certain number of hours in community service or a substance abuse education program. If someone is hurt through your actions, you could face criminal or civil charges. When out on the water, play it safe and make sure your friends do the same.

In 1995, there were:

• 836 deaths from recreational boating and 5,000 reported injuries
• 3,020 injuries from surfboarding
• 16,182 waterskiing injuries.

Source: *Accident Facts 1996*, National Safety Council

Think About It, Talk About It

1. A girl you dated a few months ago just told you she's pregnant and thinks you're the father. You're sixteen, an average student, not working, and you've never been in any trouble.

You don't want to get married, but you want to do the right thing if the baby is yours. Where do you go from here?

2. You and your friend are seventeen and talking about getting an apartment. Your parents approve, as long as you're responsible for all of your bills—and stay out of trouble!

You don't want to have to call your parents for every little thing. How do you and your friend prepare for your independence?

3. Your next-door neighbor has a tendency to "borrow" her uncle's car when he's out of town. She stops by your house in his car and offers you a ride one night.

What do you say to her?

4. You wind up at a friend's house on the other side of town, there are no adults around (they're on vacation), everyone has partied too much, and you're offered a ride home by a very tipsy friend.

You're not sure whether to accept the ride—you've also had a bit too much to drink. What's next?

Chapter 6

You and Other Important Rights

*"Make a career of humanity. Commit yourself
to the noble struggle for equal rights. You will make
a greater person of yourself, a greater nation
of your country, and a finer world to live in."*
**Martin Luther King, Jr., American civil rights leader
and Nobel Prize winner**

Laws regulate many aspects of your life—from how late you can stay out at night to whether you can sign a contract or cross the border. This chapter addresses these and many other types of rights, including the rights of gay, lesbian, and bisexual teens. You'll even read about a fifteen-year-old whose lack of telephone etiquette took him to the U.S. Supreme Court and changed the way juveniles across the nation are treated in the criminal justice system.

"Can I sign a contract?"

Most transactions today are put into writing, whether a lengthy legal contract or the fine print on a ticket stub or a store receipt. Putting an agreement in writing—between two people, two companies, or a person and a place of business—provides a record of the agreement. Everyone feels safer this way, particularly if one side doesn't follow through. But not all contracts need to be in writing to be valid. Some jobs may be done on an "as-needed" basis, and

Before you sign any document, read it carefully. Take the time to be sure you understand the terms. The fact that you're a minor may not excuse you entirely from having to comply with the contract should you later decide you want out.

no formal contract is involved. Once the work is done, payment is due. The law recognizes this type of informal agreement. Yard work, baby-sitting, and neighborhood car washes are examples.

A *contract* is defined as an agreement to do something for someone in exchange for something else. It may be between individuals, businesses, or governments. If one side fails to fulfill its part of the agreement, it's known as breaking the contract, or *breach of contract*. Generally, as a teenager, you may sue another person or business if you've been harmed or injured. Most states require that a parent, guardian, or other adult join in the lawsuit with you. Breaking a contract is a civil wrong, meaning that your case is filed in a civil, not criminal, court. The amount involved, whether $10 or $1,000,000, dictates the court where you'll file your lawsuit.

As a teenager, you may be able to enter into certain types of contracts. Your local laws tell you what kinds and under what circumstances. You may need to have a parent co-sign the contract with you. A cosigner is fully responsible if you back out of the contract or are unable to fulfill the terms.

If you're married and therefore emancipated,* you may be eligible to enter into other contracts—for example, the sale or purchase of a car or house. You can also obtain medical care and treatment for you and your spouse. That may require your signature on a medical agreement, which is a type of contract.

"Can I get out of a contract?"

The laws about contracts and minors aren't the same in every state. Because of your age and lack of business experience, you may be allowed to get out of a contract you sign. This is called

---

* See Chapter 5, pages 96–98.

disaffirming a contract, and it means you may refuse to honor its terms. The law recognizes that some businesses engage in unfair practices. Teenagers and young adults are frequent targets of scam artists and aggressive marketing campaigns.

To learn what legal protection you have, refer to your state's laws. Ask your librarian for help, or call your district attorney or attorney general's office and talk to a member of their consumer protection staff. The office may have a pamphlet to send you regarding your rights as a consumer.

In the United States, there's a "Cooling-Off Rule," also called the "Door-to-Door Sales Rule." If you buy something that costs more than $25, you have three days to cancel the purchase. The sale must take place in your home or away from the seller's regular place of business—for example, at a home party, at a restaurant, or in a rented room. The rule doesn't cover mail or telephone orders, or sales at arts and crafts fairs. Contact the Federal Trade Commission (FTC) for specifics on how to cancel a sale and deal with any problems.

FYI

Federal Trade Commission
Office of Consumer Education
Washington, DC 20580
(202) 326-3650
http://www.ftc.gov
Request the "Cooling-Off Rule" information sheet. Or read it on the Web:
http://www.ftc.gov/bcp/conline/pubs/buying/cooling.htm

If you sign a contract with an adult cosigner, you may be able to disaffirm the contract, but the cosigner remains responsible. Not all contracts you enter into may be disaffirmed. If you've obtained products or services and fail to pay for them, the provider may take you to court and might possibly involve your parents. This includes purchases involving food, clothing, lodging, and medical care.

Other large-ticket items that you've contracted for—a car, sports equipment, or stereo—may or may not be disaffirmed. You may be able to return the item without any payment to the store, or you may be required to pay for its use or any damage.

A note of caution: Before you make any out-of-the-ordinary purchase or enter into a purchase agreement, take some time to think it through. Discuss your plans with an adult, and carefully read the contract before you sign it. If you don't understand something in the contract, ask for clarification. If the salesperson is uncooperative or acts confused, walk away from the situation. If the offer seems too good to be true, it probably is. Finally, always get a copy of the contract you sign.

"What if I'm discriminated against based on my age, sex, or race?"

In 1996, a 14-year-old Texas student won a 6-year battle with his school district over his 7" ponytail.

When Zachariah was in the third grade, his school had a grooming rule that included the length of boys' hair—the restrictions didn't apply to girls. Since Zachariah's hair violated the rule, he was placed on in-school suspension for 4 months. He missed lunch, recess, gym, and other activities with his classmates. He finally withdrew from school and was taught at home.

Since his hairstyle didn't disrupt or interfere with the school's educational goals, the court determined that the rule amounted to gender discrimination.

Discrimination is defined as treating someone differently based on something other than merit, such as race, age, or gender. You might know what it feels like to be singled out or treated differently. Maybe you've had an experience at school or work. Is discrimination legal? If it isn't, what can you do about it?

It's true that teenagers can be and are discriminated against. It happens every day in many ways. You can't drive until you reach a certain age; you have to go to school between certain ages;* you can't get married or hold certain jobs until you meet the age requirements; and so on. These are

* See the chart on page 180.

lawful restrictions based on your age. Whether at school, work, or in the community, age discrimination against teenagers and other minors is legal if it's for a legitimate purpose.

In some situations, males may legally be treated differently than females. One example is the military. Although men and women may enlist in the military, most combat positions are restricted to men.

At school, most gender-based discrimination has been eliminated. Classes, clubs, and organizations are integrated, with the exception of some gym classes. Team sports have also opened up over the years to include both genders, with some ongoing debate about contact sports such as wrestling and football.

Federal and state laws have eliminated discrimination in the workplace based on race, religion, gender, and disability. Certain age restrictions are still allowed (for underage minors and the elderly). Also, employers may pay employees different wages based on job performance and length of employment.

Over the past five decades, discrimination based on race has been declared illegal in all aspects of society. The landmark Supreme Court decision in *Brown v. Board of Education* (1954) declared the "separate but equal" doctrine unconstitutional. This ruling abolished separate schools for white and African-American children. It's now illegal to discriminate on the basis of race regarding housing, public health care, public welfare services, and the military.

If you feel that you've been unlawfully discriminated against, talk with your parents. Your rights are important—no one should be allowed to violate them. Your state attorney general's office may have a civil rights division. Give them a call for information and assistance.

Discrimination by Angela Phillips (New Discovery Books, 1993). The history of discrimination and prejudice, from its first recorded appearance in A.D. 380 to present-day crises between different races, religions, and class systems.

Respecting Our Differences: A Guide to Getting Along in a Changing World by Lynn Duvall (Free Spirit Publishing, 1994). Explores the problems of discrimination, stereotypes, and prejudices and the benefits of tolerance and respect.

"What is sexual harassment?"

Test your knowledge of sexual harassment by taking this true-or-false quiz:

> T   F   Sexual harassment is a problem at school.

> T   F   Men and boys can be victims of sexual harassment.

> T   F   Charges of sexual harassment are rarely filed.

> T   F   The best way to deal with sexual harassment is to ignore it.

Except for the last statement, all of the above are true. Sexual harassment can happen anywhere, at any time, to men and women, boys and girls. It's as under-reported as date rape,* but it can't be ignored. You and your friends have rights regarding your feelings, and you have the responsibility to assert those rights.

"A sexually abusive environment inhibits, if not prevents, the harassed student from developing her full intellectual potential and receiving the most from the academic program."—11th Circuit (1996), *Davis v. Monroe County Board of Education*

Sexual harassment is defined as any unwelcome sexual advances, requests for sexual favors, and other verbal or physical conduct of a sexual nature. As Justice Potter Stewart once said about obscenity, "I may not be able to define it . . . I know it when I see it." You may not always be able to say *why* you feel uncomfortable or threatened, but the tone, facial expression, or body language of the harasser makes you a

---

* See Chapter 4, pages 79–81.

victim of sexual harassment. It's an offense of perception—if you feel the act or comment goes beyond the usual teasing or flirting, or it's more than just a compliment, let the offender know.

Since sexual harassment involves treating someone differently because of his or her gender, it's discrimination and is against the law. Girls and women are more likely to be victims than males. Harassment can happen anywhere—at school, on the job, or in the community.

If you're a victim of unwanted sexual comments or actions, do something about it. How you handle the situation is up to you. You may choose to confront the harasser or write him or her a letter. Or you can report the incident to a school official, your boss, or a business owner. A formal complaint or legal action are other possible solutions.

> In 1992, the U.S. Supreme Court decided that students can sue for sexual harassment and collect money damages if their suit is successful.
>
> In 1996, a California jury awarded a 14-year-old girl named Tianna $500,000 in her sexual harassment lawsuit against a school district. When she was 11 years old, her complaints about a sixth-grade boy harassing her were ignored by her school. The boy subjected Tianna to insults, vulgarities, and threats to beat her up. The jury concluded that schools must work to prevent sexually hostile learning environments.

Sexual Harassment by Elaine Landau (Walker and Company, 1993). Examines the many forms that sexual harassment can take, discusses instances of sexual harassment in both work and school settings, and offers suggestions on how to handle it.

Sexual Harassment and Teens: A Program for Positive Change by Susan Strauss with Pamela Espeland (Free Spirit Publishing, 1992). Causes, effects, and laws of harassment; case studies; and prevention.

Equal Employment Opportunity Commission (EEOC)
1-800-669-4000
Call the EEOC toll-free hotline for information about filing a discrimination complaint.

"What are my rights as a gay, lesbian, or bisexual teenager?"

The law doesn't distinguish between gay, lesbian, bisexual, and heterosexual (straight) teenagers. The rights and protections provided are equally applicable to all groups, whether at home, school, or work. A violation of your rights due to sexual orientation is discrimination. While not all state anti-discrimination laws specifically prohibit discrimination based on sexual orientation, due process, equal protection, and the First Amendment may be argued in your favor.

Regarding your education, your rights begin with the basic right to attend public school. You may not be excluded from enrolling or attending school because you're gay, lesbian, or bisexual. You have the right, as all students do, to be treated fairly. Your constitutional freedoms of expression and association are fully protected while at school.

This means you're free to socialize with whomever you choose or date whomever you like. You are free to write for the school paper, distribute leaflets, wear buttons, or demonstrate—as any other student is able to do. You may join or start school clubs and attend social functions, including dances. The law forbids any discrimination by extracurricular clubs or organizations. Displays of affection on campus may be restricted, but such restrictions must be applicable to all students, gay and straight alike. Under the *Tinker* test,* your activities at school may be restricted only if they disrupt the normal routine of the school or interfere with school discipline.

In 1993, Massachusetts became the first state to ban discrimination against gay and lesbian students in public schools. Students may initiate lawsuits against a school that discriminates or subjects them to harassment.

On the home front, your parents' obligation to provide for you doesn't change or end because of your sexual orientation. They can't throw you out of the house or declare you emancipated because you're gay. Their authority over you continues, just as your

---

* See Chapter 2, pages 40–42.

responsibility to obey them continues. If you and your parents are unable to agree on or discuss these issues of sexuality, family counseling should be considered.

Your rights at work may also be protected. Although no specific Federal law prohibits employment discrimination based on sexual orientation, you may assert your due process, equal protection, and First Amendment rights. State emplement laws may also support these rights.

Another area where the debate about sexual orientation continues is the military. Gays, lesbians, and bisexuals are in the armed forces, and they continue to serve their country. Since 1993, new recruits are no longer asked about their sexual orientation. This question

If you're a straight teenager, here are a few things you should keep in mind about homosexuality:

- Don't assume that someone is gay or lesbian because he or she "looks" gay or lesbian. Ask yourself: "What does that mean, anyway? Where do I get my ideas about how homosexuals look?" And don't assume that someone isn't gay, lesbian, or bisexual because he or she doesn't "look" it.
- Just because you have warm feelings about a same-sex friend doesn't mean you're gay, lesbian, or bisexual. And just because a gay or lesbian friend has warm feelings about you doesn't mean he or she wants or expects anything more than friendship.
- Some people seem to think that all gay men and lesbians are attracted to all heterosexual men and women. Ask yourself: "Are all straight women attracted to all straight men, and vice versa?"
- Don't assume that someone who's gay, lesbian, or bisexual wants to "recruit" or "convert" others to homosexuality.

was removed from the enlistment form, along with questions regarding past sexual conduct. The policy today is "Don't ask; don't tell." However, if the military finds out that you're gay, you're likely to be discharged.

Lambda Legal Defense and Education Fund
120 Wall Street
New York, NY 10005
(212) 809-8585
Information and referrals regarding issues of sexual orientation.

OutProud! The National Coalition for Gay, Lesbian, and Bisexual Youth
http://www.cyberspaces.com/outproud/
Resources for teens and schools, recommended reading, links, and more.

Parents and Friends of Lesbians and Gays (PFLAG)
1101 Fourteenth Street NW
Suite 1030
Washington, DC 20005
(202) 638-4200
http://www.pflag.org
Information and referrals to affiliated support groups and resources around the country.

You can also contact local gay, lesbian, and bisexual organizations and hotlines, and ask them about teen support groups and social organizations.

"How late can I stay out?"

Depending on your age, there are certain times when you must be in at night. These are called *curfews*—state or local laws that require you to be off the street and at home by certain hours. For example, your curfew may be 10:00 P.M. on school nights and midnight on weekends.

Curfew is usually set by your city or town, and some communities have no curfew. In Chicago, if you're under seventeen, you must be in by 11:30 P.M. on Friday and Saturday, and by 10:30 P.M. the rest of the week. In Hawaii, your curfew is 10:00 P.M. every night, unless you're sixteen. Ask your parents, local police department, or librarian for the curfew where you live.

Due to an increase in juvenile crime, especially at night, more cities are establishing curfews for minors. Some of the curfews have been tested in court and have been upheld as constitutional. Courts weigh three factors in determining if the law being challenged is legal when it only applies to minors: the particular vulnerability of children; their inability to make critical decisions in an informed, mature manner; and the importance of the parental role in raising children. All three factors have been found adequate to justify curfew laws.

CURFEW FACTS

Curfews across the U.S. differ from city to city. Examples by age:

Anchorage, Alaska
- Ages 17 and under: 10 P.M. to 6 A.M. winter weekday nights; 11 P.M. to 6 A.M. winter weekend nights; 11 P.M. to 6 A.M. summer weekday nights; midnight to 6 A.M. summer weekend nights

Cleveland, Ohio
- Age 17: midnight to 5 A.M. every night
- Ages 13–17: 11 P.M. to 5 A.M. every night
- Ages 12 and under: darkness until dawn every night
- All ages: 9 A.M. to 2 P.M. on school days

Lansing, Michigan
- Ages 13–16: midnight to 6 A.M. every night
- Ages 12 and under: 10 P.M. to 6 A.M. every night

Las Vegas, Nevada
- High school: 10 P.M. to 5 A.M. weekday nights
- Students: 11 P.M. to 5 A.M. weekend nights
- Special "Las Vegas Strip" curfew: 9 P.M. to 5 A.M. every night

Orlando, Florida
- 17 and under: Special downtown tourist district curfew is midnight to 5 A.M. every night

If you have your parents' permission to be out after curfew, or if you're with an adult, you haven't violated the law. For example, your mother may send you to the store, or you may go out with friends and family after a football game, movie, or concert. If you violate a curfew, it may mean a fine or completing some community service hours. Some police departments will give you a ticket. Others may give you a warning and take you home, or take you to a local park or police station and call your parents to

- There were over 128,000 arrests in 1994 for curfew violations; 30% of these involved persons under 15.
- 17% of violent juvenile crimes occur during typical curfew hours (10:00 P.M./midnight to 6:00 A.M.).
- 22% of violent juvenile crimes happen after school (between 2:00 P.M. and 6:00 P.M. on school days).

Source: *Juvenile Offenders and Victims: A National Report,* National Center for Juvenile Justice (1995), with 1996 *Update on Violence*

come and pick you up. In a number of cities (including Phoenix, New Orleans, Chicago, and Jacksonville), parents are being held responsible for their kids who continue to violate curfew, which may include fines and community service hours for the parents.

If you disagree with any ticket issued to you, you have the right to plead not guilty. If you go to trial and are found guilty, the penalty should be the same. A penalty is not increased because you exercised your right to fight the ticket.

"Do I need a license to go hunting or fishing?"

You may wonder why a permit or license to hunt or fish is required in the first place. Here are two good reasons:

- The revenues raised by the money spent on licenses and permits helps to support public education about hunting and fishing laws.
- Regulation by issuing permits and licenses also controls the animal and fish populations, and provides protection for endangered species.

- In **California,** no permit is needed to collect frogs for a frog-jumping contest. But if the frog dies, you may not eat it.
- If you're 14 or younger in **Idaho,** you can hunt muskrats without a license.
- In **Massachusetts,** you must be 15 before you can buy arrowheads for hunting, and 17 to get a permit for lobster fishing.
- If you're fishing in **Oregon,** be careful about what you catch. Unless you're a school, zoo, or museum, you're not allowed to keep a piranha or walking catfish.
- In **Utah,** for an $8 fee, a 6-year-old can get a license to fish for a full bag limit.

Young people under a certain age, usually fourteen or sixteen, may fish without a license. This covers fishing in most lakes and rivers. However, you may need a permit for ocean fishing. A single-day or lifetime sportfishing license is also available in many parts of the United States.

In most states, you may not hunt without a license, regardless of your age. Obey all posted signs wherever you're fishing or hunting.* The penalties for violating the fish and game laws of your state are stiff and may include the loss of your license and equipment. Contact your state game and fish department, tribal council, sporting goods store, or park ranger for information about hunting and fishing laws.

You may be required to pass a written test before obtaining a permit. Taking a firearms safety course is advisable whether you hunt or target practice. Even if it's not required, check into the classes available in your area.

"What if I see someone abusing an animal?"

Most states have laws requiring the safe and humane treatment of animals. These laws include pets that have been brought to school, so don't forget about them when school is out or during weekends and vacations. The only exception to these protection laws is the lawful hunting of game in season, when the hunter is properly licensed. Make sure you're trained in your sport.

Studies have shown that animal abuse is a symptom of a deeply disturbed person. Findings support a relationship between child abuse, animal abuse, and domestic violence. Research in this area continues, while efforts are underway to cross-train child welfare and animal welfare professionals.

- Hitting a police horse in **Minnesota** is punishable by 2 years in jail or a $4,000 fine.
- Dognapping and catnapping are illegal in **Wisconsin.**
- In **Vermont,** dyeing or coloring baby chicks is against the law.

A person found guilty of animal abuse may be sent to jail or heavily fined. If you see someone abusing an animal, tell a responsible adult what happened. You may then decide to report the incident to the police, the local humane society, or an animal control office.

* See Chapter 7, pages 147–148.

Humane Society of the United States
2100 L St. NW
Washington, DC 20037
(202) 452-1100
http://www.hsus.org/
Contact your local humane society or the national organization for
information about pet adoption and ways to help abused, abandoned,
or neglected animals.

"Can I go across the border
with my friends?"

You may be allowed to cross national borders without your parents. During the summer, winter vacation, or spring break, many students take school trips across the border to Mexico or Canada without their parents along.

Whether you're on a school trip or visiting a border town for a day, you'll need some form of identification. You don't need a passport or visa, just verification that you're an American citizen. A driver's license or birth certificate is usually acceptable. If you're under eighteen, take along a written statement from your parents, authorizing emergency medical care. This is called a *power of attorney,* and it may save you from additional pain and aggravation. It might possibly save your life. (See page 134 for an example of a basic form.)

When traveling abroad, remember that the laws of the United States no longer apply. Make sure you know what's allowed and what isn't before you go. The penalties for violating the law may be far more severe than you'd expect in the United States. For example, in 1994, an American student traveling in Singapore was caught spray-painting cars. Authorities in Singapore punished him by caning his rear end.

Before your trip, make sure you know the curfew hours, legal drinking age, and traffic laws (including insurance requirements) of the nation you're visiting. Also be aware of whom you should contact and procedures you should follow in case of an emergency.

"Can I get into trouble for swearing?"

Depending on the circumstances, using profanity or offensive hand gestures may cause serious problems for you. In some parts of the country, you could be charged with disturbing the peace or violating a local profanity law. At school, you could be suspended or disciplined with an after-school detention or additional homework. Your parents may be called and told of the incident.

> "It is a highly appropriate function of public school education to prohibit the use of vulgar and offensive terms in public discourse." —U.S. Supreme Court (1986), *Bethel School District v. Fraser*

- A Missouri law against cursing in public was determined to be a violation of the right of free speech. A customer at a taco restaurant became upset and swore at an employee because the taco sauce was too hot. He was fined $100. The appellate court said that if the profane, indecent, or vulgar language constitutes fighting words, it could be restricted. Otherwise, it couldn't. So the customer didn't have to pay the fine.
- In 1996, 16-year-old LaTosha was ordered to spend 3 days on the sidewalk counting cars as punishment for swearing at her Texas high school nurse. LaTosha stated that she felt embarrassed "in front of all these people. . . . All my friends will see me out here."

"Can I get into trouble by using the telephone?"

When Gerald Gault was fifteen years old, he made an obscene telephone call. The call was traced to Gerald's house in Globe, Arizona. He was taken into custody, prosecuted, and placed in the state's school for boys. This is an extreme but true example of the consequences for telephone harassment. This case ended up in the U.S. Supreme Court and led to a 1967 decision that changed the rights of all minors.

Before the now famous *Gault* decision, juveniles who got into trouble with the police had very few rights. They were treated more like property belonging to their parents. As a result of *Gault*,

Power of Attorney Form

I, _____ , the _____ of
            (name)   (mother/father)

_____ , date of birth _____ ,
       (name of minor)

do hereby authorize _____
                                (name of custodian)

to obtain and sign for necessary medical care and treatment

for _____ .
                (name of minor)

[You may add any particulars that apply to the situation; for example: location, length of stay, and date of return.]

_____   _____
       Signature   Date

_____
        Notary

NOTE: This is an example of a basic power-of-attorney form—it's not an official form. State laws differ regarding the specifics. Consult an attorney, legal stationer, or law library for the appropriate form in your state.

the Supreme Court stated that children enjoy identical rights in the criminal system as adults. This includes the right to remain silent, the right to a lawyer if you're unable to afford one, the right to receive a notice of the charges filed against you, and the right to face your accuser in a court of law.

Laws regarding telephone use haven't changed since Gerald's call. Using a telephone to harass, annoy, scare, threaten, or swear at someone is, in most states, against the law. If caught, you'll be explaining yourself to a judge.

If you're a victim of telephone harassment, tell your parents. Write down the date and time of the call, and what was said. By taking immediate action, you can put an end to the harassment and assist in identifying the caller. The police and telephone company may get involved if the calls continue.

"Can I buy and use fireworks?"

When used carelessly or by people under the influence of alcohol or drugs, fireworks can quickly turn a celebration into a disaster. In 1992, there were two deaths in the United States from fireworks; there were ten deaths in 1993.*

Before handling or buying fireworks, find out what's legal in your city or town. The police or fire department can give you specific information. In most states, fireworks are subject to restrictions. In California, for example,

- In **Massachusetts,** selling a stink bomb that "gives off a foul odor" carries a $10 to $200 fine.
- In **North Dakota,** only certain fireworks may be sold to children who are at least 12 years old, and only between June 27 and July 5. These include sparklers, wheels, fountains, star lights, helicopter flyers, torches, comets, and soft-shell firecrackers.

you must be eighteen to use or possess dangerous fireworks, including firecrackers, skyrockets, ground spinners, roman candles, sparklers longer than ten inches, any exploding device, and many others. "Safe and sane" fireworks (which include anything not classified as "dangerous") may be used if you're sixteen.

---

* **Source:** *Accident Facts 1996,* National Safety Council

Think About It, Talk About It

1. While your parents are out, a teenager comes to your door selling magazine subscriptions. Some of the magazines look interesting to you, and $45 for a year's subscription to three magazines seems too good to pass up, so you sign a form agreeing to the deal. Later, when you tell your parents, they insist that you get out of the agreement.

Now what do you do?

2. It's 11:55 P.M. on a Friday night. Curfew is midnight, and you and your friends are walking home—another fifteen minutes away. You're stopped by the police, who question you about your age and what you're doing. It's now after midnight, and you're given a curfew ticket.

What do you think? Did you violate curfew? Do you think you'll be able to convince a judge that you would have been home by midnight? How would you prevent this from happening again?

3. Tiffany was fifteen when she started her freshman year at a high school in Kansas. In eighth grade, she had been a member of her junior high wrestling team, with a record of five wins and three losses. She wanted to try out for her high school wrestling team but was prohibited because she was a girl. The school explained that there were concerns about her safety, potential disruption in the school setting, possible sexual harassment issues, and some inconvenience to the wrestling program. Tiffany and her mother sued the principal, the coach, and the school district, charging them with violating her right to equal protection of the law. In 1996, a federal court agreed with Tiffany. The school was ordered to let her try out and participate if she made the wrestling team. The school's concerns were determined minimal compared with the personal loss of opportunity for Tiffany.

Do you agree with the decision? Why or why not? Should gender be a consideration in sports at school?

Chapter 7

Crimes and Punishments

"When in doubt, tell the truth."
Mark Twain, American author

Now that you know your rights and responsibilities, you might want to know the consequences of breaking the law. In the next two chapters, you'll learn about your involvement with the legal system—from the point of being charged with a criminal offense, to your rights following a conviction and sentence.

Less than 1 percent of America's juveniles ages ten to seventeen were arrested in 1994 for violent crimes including murder, rape, assault, and robbery. Of the total population of 27 million kids in the U.S. between the ages of ten and seventeen, about 150,000 were arrested. Most teens are law-abiding citizens, but the few violent offenders have focused the nation's attention on all youth. You don't need to look too far for another

- Between 1990 and 1994, adult crime *decreased*, including violent crime (murder, rape, assault, and robbery). But juvenile violent crime *increased*. Approximately 4,000 murders were committed each year by persons under 18.
- Between 1985 and 1994, juvenile arrests for murder *increased* 150%.
- The overall number of juveniles between ages 15 and 17 is expected to increase 31% by the year 2010. If the crime rate of the past 10 years continues, juvenile arrests for violent crime will double to more than 300,000 a year.
- Teenage girls committed 25% of all juvenile crime in 1995, with 701,800 girls under 18 arrested.

Source: *Juvenile Offenders and Victims: A National Report*, National Center for Juvenile Justice (1995), with *1996 Update on Violence*

story about a gang killing, drive-by shooting, drug bust, or sexual assault involving a teen offender.

Statistics* indicate that in 1994, juveniles were responsible for:

- 10 percent of all murders
- 13 percent of all aggravated assaults
- 14 percent of all forcible rapes
- 20 percent of all robberies
- 21 percent of all burglaries
- 25 percent of all larceny thefts
- 25 percent of all motor vehicle thefts
- 48 percent of all arsons.

It's important for you to know the terminology and consequences of illegal behavior. Criminal law, once applicable only to adults, now applies to you; there's only one set of criminal laws in each state, and they pertain to teens and adults alike. The language and procedures may differ between the adult and juvenile systems, but the basic criminal law is the same.

To find out more about teens, crime, and its consequences, consider inviting a police officer, prosecutor, defense attorney, or judge to speak to your social studies class. He or she could discuss the laws that apply to you, as well as the philosophy of criminal justice in America. Many police departments, prosecutors, and public defender offices have a community relations person you can contact to arrange for a speaker.

Do you know the difference between a felony and a misdemeanor? Do you know the difference between being charged as a delinquent and an incorrigible child? What about the laws regarding fighting at home or school, or joining a gang? You're probably familiar with the restrictions on alcohol and drugs, but did you know that having a juvenile record for substance abuse may follow you around as an adult?

---

* **Source:** *Juvenile Offenders and Victims: A National Report,* National Center for Juvenile Justice (1995), with 1996 *Update on Violence*

"What's the difference between a felony and a misdemeanor?"

"High crimes and misdemeanors," "petty and status offenses," "city ordinances," "felonies," "infractions"—you've probably heard many, if not all, of these terms. Through TV, the movies, or personal experience, you've come across these references to crime. But what exactly are they, and what do they mean to you?

Crime is divided into categories: *felonies, misdemeanors,* and *petty offenses.* If a crime is committed by a minor, it's referred to as a *delinquent act.* The seriousness of the act determines its classification and the resulting penalty.

A felony is the most serious crime. Felonies include murder, assault, residential burglary, kidnapping, and other violent offenses. The penalty for conviction of a felony may include jail in excess of one year, probation, prison, a life sentence, or death.

- Juveniles accounted for 19% of all violent crime arrests in 1994.
- In 1994, there were 322,000 juvenile arrests for misdemeanor offenses, including vandalism and disorderly conduct, and 128,000 arrests for the petty offenses of curfew and loitering.

Source: *Juvenile Offenders and Victims: A National Report*, National Center for Juvenile Justice (1995), with 1996 *Update on Violence*

A misdemeanor isn't as serious as a felony. Conviction may result in a jail term, usually up to one year. You may also be placed on probation with specific terms such as counseling, drug tests, or community service hours. Misdemeanor offenses include shoplifting, trespassing, criminal damage, and disorderly conduct.

A petty offense or *infraction* is any violation of the law that isn't designated a misdemeanor or a felony. These are lesser offenses such as underage smoking, seat belt violations, or littering. They usually result in a small fine. A *status offense* is any act committed by an underage person that wouldn't be an offense if committed by an adult. Runaway incidents, curfew violations, possession of alcohol or tobacco, and truancy are all examples of status offenses. These acts are against the law only because you're a minor.

"What is a juvenile delinquent?"

Words and phrases differ between the juvenile and adult justice systems. There's a long-standing philosophy that children who break the law are to be nurtured and rehabilitated, not punished as criminals. Consequently, the language isn't as harsh when referring to a juvenile offender. Here's how the two "languages" compare:

In the juvenile system . . .	In the adult system . . .
juvenile	defendant
adjudication hearing	trial
disposition hearing	sentencing
detention	jail
department of juvenile corrections	prison
delinquent act	crime
delinquent	criminal

There's only one set of criminal laws in each state, and it applies to everyone. However, when a child breaks one of these laws, he or she is dealt with in the juvenile justice system.

Another term closely associated with delinquency is *incorrigibility*. This only applies to minors—anyone under the age of majority (eighteen in most states). Any minor found guilty of a status offense is considered an incorrigible child.

If you're a truant, a runaway, disobedient, a curfew violator, or someone who uses or possesses alcohol or tobacco products, you may be declared by the court to be incorrigible. If this happens, you may be placed on probation for a period of time, usually six to twelve months. Whatever the problems and issues are at home,

- In 1993, there were 34,000 truancy cases filed, with 78% of those found guilty put on probation.
- In the same year, 16,000 juveniles were charged as incorrigibles, with 63% placed on probation.
- In 1994, Washington, D.C., New York, Florida, California, New Jersey, and Maryland had the highest juvenile arrest rates for 10- to 17-year-olds (for murder, rape, robbery, and assault).

Source: *Juvenile Offenders and Victims: A National Report*, National Center for Juvenile Justice (1995), with 1996 *Update on Violence*

services will be provided to help you change things. If you're ever in this situation, work with the counselors and probation officers so you can get on with your life.

More and more states are expecting parents to exercise control over their children. Parental responsibility laws are being passed, and they carry civil and criminal penalties for violation. In 1996, the parents of a teenager in Michigan were found guilty of parental irresponsibility in supervising their son. Sixteen-year-old Alex was described as a one-boy crime wave. In his bedroom were a stolen gun, alcohol, and marijuana plants. He burglarized churches and threatened his father with a golf club. Alex was sentenced to one year in lockup, while his parents were fined $100 each and ordered to pay $1,000 in court costs.

Can You Name These Celebrity Delinquents?

1. She was eighteen when she was arrested in Florida in 1994 for possession of marijuana. She entered a drug treatment program and returned to tennis later that year. No charges were filed.

2. He was a shy, stuttering child, adopted as a baby. He started diving at age nine. He battled low self-esteem, bouts of depression, drugs and alcohol, and conflicts over his sexual orientation. He considered suicide at twelve and was later arrested and placed in detention for three days for kicking his mother. He turned his life around and at sixteen won an Olympic silver medal. He went on to win four gold medals and numerous world championships.

3. He was twenty-five years old when he was arrested in Michigan in 1978 on drug charges. He was convicted and sentenced to three to seven years in prison. He spent his time reading, took a public speaking course, and worked on a comedy routine.

Answers: 1. Jennifer Capriati, tennis star; 2. Greg Louganis, Olympic diver; 3. Tim Allen, star of TV's *Home Improvement*

"Am I in trouble with the law if I disobey my parents?"

Behavior that at one time was considered fun and mischievous—or just part of growing up—is now reason for you and your parents to appear in court. An overnight with a friend that turns into several days may be viewed as a runaway act, a night out on the town may land you a curfew violation, and senior "ditch day" is considered truancy. These are examples of status offenses, and they can only be committed by someone under eighteen.

Your parents are required to provide for your care and upbringing. You, in turn, are required to obey them and follow their rules. The law gives parents a lot of freedom in raising families. It's not unlimited, however. If the rules of the house are reasonable under the law—even if they don't seem reasonable to you—they must be followed. If the rules place you in danger of being neglected or abused, however, you need to report what's going on and get help for yourself and your brothers and sisters.*

- 248,000 juveniles were arrested in 1994 as runaways; 57% were girls under 18, and 45% were under 15.
- 34% of runaways have run away at least once in the previous year; 16% went more than 50 miles from home.
- Over 59,000 children each year are "thrown away," told to leave home, abandoned, or not claimed when picked up as runaways.

Source: *Juvenile Offenders and Victims: A National Report,* National Center for Juvenile Justice (1995), with 1996 *Update on Violence*

Parents who've tried punishments (such as grounding or loss of privileges) and have failed to improve their child's behavior can file an incorrigibility charge against their child. A judge will then decide what to do, from putting the child on probation to ordering counseling or locking the child up for a period of time.

Disorderly conduct is another act that's against the law. It's sometimes called *disturbing the peace,* and it happens when you act in a way that upsets someone else. Examples include fighting, making

---

* See Chapter 4, pages 74–76, for more information on abuse and neglect.

loud noise, cursing, disruptive behavior in public, or refusing to obey an order from a police officer, firefighter, or school official. It's also possible to disturb the peace at home. If you're disruptive and your parents' peace is upset, you may end up in court.

Approximately one million children run away from home each year. Another 300,000 children are homeless, living on the streets with no supervision, nurturance, or regular assistance from a parent or responsible adult. Many more youth are homeless along with their families. If you or a friend needs help or someone to talk to in a difficult situation, call the operator or 911 for immediate assistance, or call a hotline for counseling or referrals in your community.

Covenant House Nineline
1-800-999-9999
http://www.covenanthouse.org
Immediate help in crisis situations. Ask about Operation Home Free, which provides free transportation home for runaways.

National Runaway Hotline
1-800-231-6946
All calls are confidential.

National Runaway Switchboard
1-800-621-4000
A referral service for youth in personal crisis.

"What will happen to me if I get caught shoplifting?"

Scene One: After school, Julie, Colin, and Matt stop at the local store for a snack and something to drink. Julie is by herself for a few seconds, and she slips a pack of gum into her pocket, knowing that she doesn't have enough money to pay for all of the items she wants. She pays for her chips and drink and leaves the store with her friends.

Scene Two: Julie, Colin, and Matt only have 60 cents between them. They stop at the store, and while Matt keeps the car running, Julie and Colin enter the store. While Colin distracts the clerk, Julie puts a six-pack of beer in her backpack. They leave the store and begin to party at a nearby park.

Shoplifting is defined as taking property that's displayed for sale, without paying for it. It's a crime with both civil and criminal consequences. It's also a crime that requires *intent*. If you were shopping and put something in your pocket, continued shopping, went to the checkout, and paid for everything but the item in your pocket, you could be questioned about your intentions. If it turned out that you had the money to pay for the item and didn't act or look suspicious during the incident, you would probably be allowed to leave. Otherwise, you could be held for further questioning or for the police.

Scene One above presents a different picture. Julie knew that she didn't have enough money for everything she wanted, so she stole the gum and paid for the rest. This is shoplifting, and since her friends didn't know or play any part in the incident, they would be free to go if caught by the store owner.

Scene Two is your classic "beer run," where all involved know exactly what's happening and what their role is. Just because Julie took the beer doesn't mean the others won't be prosecuted if caught. Under the law, anyone aiding a crime shares full responsibility, just as if he or she had actually committed the act. Julie, Colin, and Matt could all be charged with shoplifting and possession of alcohol.

In many jurisdictions, a store can collect a civil penalty, plus the cost of the item taken, from the shoplifter or his or her parents. For example, the civil penalty for the stolen six-pack could be $100, plus the retail cost of the beer.

In **Washington,** if you don't pay your restaurant bill, your parents may be responsible for up to $500.

If you shoplift, the police may send their report to the local prosecutor, who decides whether to file charges. If filed, you'll be in court facing possible detention or probation. First-time shoplifters usually go through a diversion program, which includes counseling, community service hours, and restitution. If you're caught a second time, probation may be considered, with specific terms set by the court. If you continue to steal, it's possible you'll receive detention or placement with the state department of juvenile corrections.

Shoplifters Anonymous
1-800-848-9595
Call to request printed materials or audiocassettes for a home-study program.

"Is it against the law to fight?"

Your everyday spat between siblings isn't against the law. But if the argument escalates and someone is injured, the law has been broken. Fighting is referred to by different names, depending on the incident and whether injuries occur. *Assault, disorderly conduct,* or *disturbing the peace* are terms often used to describe an exchange of words or blows with another person.

Let's say you're at home after school, and your sister walks in wearing your new shoes. She didn't ask to borrow them, and now they're scuffed up. You start yelling at each other, and you get angrier when she argues that *you* do the same thing with *her* clothes. You grab the TV remote control, throw it, and it hits her on the head.

This is an example of a verbal fight that turned into an assault. You weren't threatened by your sister, so you can't claim self-defense. If you're the aggressor and made the first contact, you may be charged with assault.

Assume that this confrontation lasts for a while or goes on all night. Your father is home, he's unable to control the two of you, and he becomes increasingly upset over the situation. Your acts have disturbed your father's peace and quiet. Both you and your sister could be charged with disorderly conduct.

You're a victim of disorderly conduct if someone near you disrupts your peace by fighting, exhibiting violent behavior, swearing, or making loud noise. Or you could get involved in an after-school fight behind the gym or under the bleachers. Mutual combat—in which you and another person or persons agree to fight—may be disorderly conduct or a violation of a local law. It's clearly against school policy, requiring you to face disciplinary action by the school. If you're trained in boxing or the martial arts, your level of proficiency may be considered by the court and could increase any consequences imposed, depending on the circumstances of the case.

A recent national survey showed that girls ages 9–14 are as violent as boys:

- 66% said they had seen 1–10 fights during the past year; 10% had witnessed more than 10 fights.
- 36% had been in physical fights during the past year. 33% fought another girl; 30% fought a boy.
- 72% had "seen or heard" of girls who carry weapons; 17% carried weapons themselves.

The girls gave these reasons for being violent:

- they've been victims of violence themselves (54%)
- they want to look tough (50%)
- they don't have a good family life (43%)
- they want to get even with someone (41%)
- they need to protect themselves (38%).

Source: "Girls Talk About Violence," a national survey of about 500 young women by the Center for Women Policy Studies, a nonprofit policy-research and advocacy organization in Washington, D.C.

Random fighting takes place on school grounds from elementary school through the twelfth grade. In 1996, a three-year-old schoolyard bully in Boston was ordered by a judge to stop hitting a classmate and was told that if he continued hitting, he could face a fine or jail. Kids are resorting to violence more often when faced with a challenge. A wrong look or comment, offensive colors or styles of clothing, or unintentional contact with someone in the hall may spark a confrontation.

Many schools and communities now offer classes in conflict resolution. If your school doesn't offer this kind of program, see if you can help set something up. Trained professionals are available in most communities and may be willing to speak to students and teachers. Check with your local police department or domestic violence shelters for more information.

"What is trespassing?"

"Do Not Enter," "Private Property," "No Trespassing." You've probably seen these signs on vacant lots, wooded areas, abandoned houses, or near factories. *Trespass* is defined as entering or remaining on someone's property without permission. If there's a sign posted (whether you see it or not), or if you've been told by the owner not to be on the property, this is considered adequate notice. Disregarding these rules can result in a charge of trespass, which is a misdemeanor.

It's not always necessary to post a "No Trespassing" sign. If the owner of the property or a security officer tells you to leave and not return, that's notice enough. If you return, you're trespassing. If you're disruptive at a mall and a security guard tells you to leave and not return, you must do so. As long as you're not excluded based on race, gender, religion, or disability, the restriction placed on you is valid.

Other places that are off-limits include mines, railroad cars and tracks, and fenced commercial yards. If a property is fenced, it's a good indication that you need permission to be there. This includes fenced property in rural areas where you might want to hunt or target practice. Places that aren't as obvious include your neighbor's yard or pool, school grounds when school is out, or church property and parks when they're closed. Someone's car or garage are off limits, unless you have permission. If you're ever in doubt about whether you're trespassing,

- In **Hawaii,** no minors are allowed in dance halls where paid partners are available.
- If you're caught peeking into someone's window in **South Dakota,** you'll be explaining why to a judge.
- If you're under 16 in **Washington,** you must be with a parent or guardian at an outdoor music festival. If you're not, you could be charged with trespassing and/or a curfew violation, depending on the time of day.

keep your eyes open for posted signs or ask for permission from the property owner.

"What if I start a fire that gets out of control?"

Most fires are either accidental or acts of nature: defective wiring or appliances, lightning, campfires, or explosions. A number of fires, though, are intentionally set. Depending on the amount of damage and the exact cause, these fires constitute crimes called *arson* or *reckless burning.*

- Over 11,000 juveniles were arrested in 1994 for arson.
- 12% of those arrested were female, and 68% were under age 15.

Source: *Juvenile Offenders and Victims: A National Report,* National Center for Juvenile Justice (1995), with 1996 *Update on Violence*

Arson is defined as unlawfully and knowingly damaging property by causing a fire or explosion. Reckless burning is recklessly causing a fire or explosion that results in property damage. You may not have intended to damage anything, but your behavior was careless and reckless. For example, making a firebomb or any explosive device is dangerous and illegal. Whether a fire was intentional or not, you and your parents may have to pay all or part of the damage you caused.

If you find yourself in a fire situation and are unsure what to do, ask for help immediately by dialing the operator or 911, or contact your fire department.

"What if I damage someone else's property?"

If you damage property, it makes little difference whether it was a car, home, school, or business. And it doesn't matter whether the act was intentional or not. The issue becomes one of accountability and restitution. If the act is intentional or malicious, it's called *vandalism,* which is a misdemeanor or a felony, depending on the amount of damage. Otherwise, it's called *criminal damage.*

In 1994, 152,000 juveniles were arrested for vandalism. But most cases of property damage are accidental or careless. Some states set a limit on how much your parents have to pay for your acts of property damage, but it may be as high as $10,000. Other states have no limit, which means that you and your parents are responsible for paying for *all* damages.

- In Arizona, a 16-year-old who spray-painted 32 homes, a half-dozen cars, and various garage doors and fences was tried as an adult and sentenced to 2 months in jail and 3 years probation.
- Two teenagers in New Jersey were charged in federal court with painting swastikas on headstones in a Jewish cemetery. Kevin, 18, was sentenced to 15 months in prison; Chris, 19, was sentenced to 12 months.

Defacing property means marking, scratching, or painting (tagging) property that doesn't belong to you without the owner's permission. For example, if you paint graffiti on your neighbor's car or fence, you've broken the law and are responsible for the repairs. Some cities are putting taggers to work removing or painting over graffiti.

States with major graffiti problems have passed laws that have serious penalties. In California, a second offense carries a $1,000 fine and six months in jail. If the child is unable to pay the fine, his or her parents are responsible. Texas has a similar statute. Rhode Island limits the use and possession of spray paint to those over eighteen, unless approved by the parents. Graffiti artists in Florida may lose their driver's license for up to one year.

"Is it illegal to belong to a gang?"

It's not against the law to be a member of a gang. The First Amendment's freedom of assembly gives you the right to join any group or club, assuming you meet their requirements. Membership in the Ku Klux Klan, a neo-Nazi group, or a white supremacist

Belonging to a club or organization isn't against the law, and there are many reasons to join a group. But you can draw your own conclusions and decide for yourself if gang life is for you. Consider these facts:

- 50% of gang-related crimes involve a homicide or other violence, due mainly to defense of territory, retaliation, witness intimidation, or graffiti.
- The presence of fighting gangs in schools increased 20% between 1989 and 1993.
- 62% of students at schools with gangs report seeing weapons on campus.

Source: *Juvenile Offenders and Victims: A National Report,* National Center for Juvenile Justice (1995), with 1996 *Update on Violence*

organization isn't illegal. The individual acts of a member may be unlawful, but not the mere fact of membership.

Gang-related shootings, stabbings, and violence connected with drugs and alcohol happen every day. Schools, law enforcement agencies, and community organizations are working together to confront this problem. Los Angeles, for example, has the After School Alternative Program (ASAP) to help young people make better use of their time after school until a parent gets home from work. Legislatures have also passed stricter laws regarding gang activities, with increased penalties for gang crimes.

"Can I gamble? What if I win the lottery?"

"You wanna bet?" "Put your money where your mouth is." "I'll bet you $5 I'm right." Everyone has said something like this at one time or another. Most of the time, you're kidding. However, if you're serious and you expect to collect on a bet or pay it off if you lose, you may have broken the law.

In most states, minors may not bet, gamble, or be in a bar or saloon where gambling occurs. This includes betting at a horse or dog track, buying a lottery ticket, or any type of gambling (with dice, cards, or other games of chance). These rules generally apply, even in some states with

- The presence of children at a racetrack or offtrack betting location is forbidden in **Connecticut.**
- In **Delaware,** you must be 21 to play a video lottery machine but only 18 to buy a lottery ticket.

legalized gambling. The exchange of money or property is considered unlawful when it comes to minors.

Although you must be an adult to gamble, you can receive lottery tickets as a gift. If you win, you may be allowed to keep part of the prize, depending on the amount. States vary on this—some give you a percent of the total amount, while others require that the money be paid to your parents or guardians.

• In 1994, 1,700 males and females under 18 were arrested for gambling.
• Over the 10-year period from 1985–1994, the increase in female arrests for gambling (145%) exceeded the male arrest increase (96%).

Source: *Juvenile Offenders and Victims: A National Report,* National Center for Juvenile Justice (1995), with 1996 *Update on Violence*

Some of the symptoms of becoming a compulsive gambler to watch for include:

• a growing preoccupation with gambling
• gambling greater amounts over a longer period
• increased restlessness when not gambling
• gambling more to win back your losses
• missing school or work to gamble
• growing debt.

If you or a friend have developed a habit of gambling and the situation is getting out of hand, contact Gamblers Anonymous. Check your local phone book for a listing. Some groups have programs for teens.

FYI

Gamblers Anonymous
International Service Office
P. O. Box 17173
Los Angeles, CA 90017
(213) 386-8789
http://www.gamblersanonymous.org/

National Council on Compulsive Gambling
1-800-522-4700
Information and referrals to a Gamblers Anonymous or Gam-Anon (loved ones of gambling addicts) group in your area.

"What if I use a fake ID?"

This looks like the real thing, doesn't it? Actually, it is. It's an identification card showing the real cardholder, but the statistics are false. Peter's birthdate is wrong, as well as the phone number. When Peter bought this for five dollars at a park-'n'-swap, he was only seventeen years old. He successfully passed himself off as twenty-one and was able to buy beer on several occasions. Then one night a liquor store clerk asked Peter for additional ID, which he didn't have. Peter was caught.

Using a fake ID is against the law and is either a misdemeanor or petty offense. It doesn't make any difference why you're using it or where. You may be trying to get into an age-restricted club, movie, or pool hall, or even enlist in the armed forces.

If you're caught using a fake ID and don't admit to your acts, an additional charge of *false reporting* may be filed. Any attempt to mislead a police officer to avoid getting into trouble usually backfires. Law enforcement and the courts take into consideration your statements when first contacted by the police. If you break the law, you're better off being honest and straightforward when questioned.

Think About It, Talk About It

1. You may have told yourself, "What's the big deal about shoplifting? It's so easy to do, especially in a crowded store. I've never been caught, plus the store makes so much money—what I take doesn't hurt them." Why do you think the penalties for shoplifting are so stiff?

2. You're at a party at your friend's house while her parents are away for the weekend. After a few beers, you somehow manage to break her mom's favorite vase.

You feel guilty and want to do the right thing, but you don't want to get your friend in trouble for having the party. What should you do?

3. It seems like everyone on your block belongs to a gang known as the Southside Sharks. They want you to join them, and you're scared to say no.

You're afraid you'll get cut up or beat up no matter what you decide. What should you do?

4. A friend of yours has a fake ID. When you confront him about it, he says, "It's fun to have, and sometimes it works. I'm not hurting anyone by using it."

Is he right?

Chapter 8

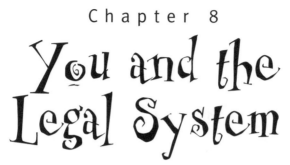

You and the Legal System

"The language of the law must not be foreign to those who are to obey it."

Learned Hand, American jurist who ruled in almost 3,000 cases

At some point in your life, you may be involved in a lawsuit or have to appear in court. You may get sued, be a defendant in a criminal trial, or get called to court as a witness or a juror. Or maybe you'll study to become a paralegal, attorney, or one of the many other professional members of the legal community. Whatever the case, you'll need a basic knowledge of the legal system. This final chapter will give you a head start.

If you've followed any high-profile court case in the news, you already have some familiarity with the legal system. At first glance, it may appear complicated, but you'll see that it's logical and, for the most part, based on common sense. The mysteries that surround the Latin terms and legal theories aren't difficult to solve.

This chapter will give you an understanding of the court system, the nature of a lawsuit, and

- In 1995, more than 22,000 new state laws were passed.
- There are over 16,000 trial and appellate courts in the U.S.
- In 1994, almost 2 million delinquency (breaking the law) cases were processed in the nation's juvenile courts. 329,000 juveniles were placed on probation, and 11,800 were transferred to adult court.

Sources: *The National Law Journal,* 1/22/96; National Center for State Courts; *Juvenile Offenders and Victims: A National Report,* National Center for Juvenile Justice (1995), with 1996 *Update on Violence*

the function of a jury. You'll see the distinctions between a juvenile and adult court, as well as the purpose for transferring some teenagers under eighteen to the adult criminal system. You'll also learn about the ultimate consequences of breaking the law: a life sentence or capital punishment. Did you know that if you're sixteen, you're eligible for a cell on death row?

"What is a lawsuit?"

Have you ever worked for someone, baby-sat, or done yard work and not been paid? Was your first car a lemon and the seller refused to do anything about it?

If your answer to either of these questions is yes, you may have a lawsuit on your hands. A *civil lawsuit* is a disagreement with someone about property, personal behavior, injury, or any activity that affects your rights. A *criminal lawsuit* can only be filed by the government—by a prosecutor. This isn't a private suit, with one person against another or against a company. A criminal suit pits the government (city, state, etc.) against an individual.

In your civil dispute, if all attempts to resolve the issue fail, you may ask a court to settle it through a lawsuit. With the help of your parents, guardian, or attorney, you may be able to sue the person or company that violated your rights. Generally, until you're an adult, you can't file a lawsuit by yourself. A *next friend* must file the suit on your behalf.

Once the lawsuit is filed, the court, with or without a jury, decides the case after considering the evidence and the arguments of both attorneys. You and your opponent are required to follow the court's decision.

Millions of lawsuits are filed in the United States each year. Some take years to settle or get to trial. *Alternate dispute resolution* (ADR) is a process of settling many of these lawsuits without waiting for your day in court. The trend in all areas of litigation, with the exception of criminal prosecution, includes some form of ADR.

A similar practice called *plea bargaining* exists in criminal cases. This occurs when the prosecutor offers to reduce the charge against you if you agree to admit to the reduced charge. Let's say you're caught breaking into someone's house and stealing $50. The prosecutor files two charges against you—burglary and theft. The "bargain" offered is your admission to one of the charges in return for dismissal of the other. This is a common and necessary practice in criminal and delinquency cases. There are too many cases filed for each to go to trial, and the offender's rehabilitation and treatment can begin sooner if a plea bargain is accepted.

Everyone has the right to go to court to ask for help in resolving a dispute. However, when this right is abused, the court may limit its access. For example, an inmate in West Virginia, serving a life sentence for murder, filed 5 lawsuits seeking hundreds of thousands of dollars in damages. He claimed injury for such incidents as glass in his yogurt, an exploding television, and an exploding can of shaving cream! All of his lawsuits were thrown out of court as frivolous, and restrictions were placed on his use of typewriters and computers.

Mediation and *arbitration* are two methods of dispute resolution that have become increasingly popular around the nation. You may have experienced similar methods at school in settling disputes with other students. Mediation involves a neutral third person who assists the parties in the lawsuit to reach a compromise. Suggestions and proposals regarding settlement are made. If an agreement can't be reached, the parties may agree to take the next step—arbitration—or go to trial.

In arbitration, the parties to the lawsuit agree in advance to let a third person consider the case and decide the issues. You and your attorney meet with the arbitrator and your opponents. The case is discussed, both sides present their evidence and arguments, and the arbitrator reaches a decision. The arbitrator is usually someone who has knowledge and experience in the area concerning the lawsuit. He or she is generally trained in arbitration skills. Hundreds of cases are settled this way, saving time, money, and aggravation.

If all attempts at resolution fail and you're considering filing a lawsuit, make sure the time limit hasn't expired. A *statute of*

• *Hogan's Heroes* star Bob Crane was murdered in 1978, but his killer wasn't arrested and prosecuted until 1992.
• While fishing in Canada with his father and brothers in 1971, Wayne R. confessed to killing his 4-year-old stepdaughter and burying her in Arizona. After 25 years, the family secret was revealed, and Wayne was convicted of murder.

limitations requires that lawsuits be filed within a specified time (two years, for example). If you go past the deadline, you won't be able to pursue your rights. This law applies to both civil and criminal cases, with a few exceptions in criminal law (murder and treason, for example, have no statute of limitations). These crimes may be charged at any time, even twenty to thirty years after the incident.

"Why are there so many different courts?"

Throughout the United States, there are courts with different responsibilities and authority. The courts derive their authority from state and federal constitutions, and from laws passed by state legislatures. Each court has specific cases that it can hear, as well as a higher court *(appellate court),* which reviews lower court decisions. This is referred to as a court's *jurisdiction.* For example, a justice or municipal court may only deal with misdemeanor violations of city laws or small-dollar civil lawsuits, not felonies or high-dollar cases.

There are basically two court systems in the United States: *federal* and *state.* Each is divided into three levels. The lowest is the *trial court,* and the second and third levels are *appellate courts.* Various lower courts exist, such as the *municipal court, justice court,* and *police court.* Each of these has specific subject matter jurisdictions. Only those cases that the law designates may be heard in each court.

The basic structure of the court system remains stable—trial courts with one or two levels of appellate courts. However, with a growing population and an increase in the number of lawsuits filed, more judges and courts are needed at all levels.

In trial courts and lower courts, juries are called to hear the evidence and decide the case. At the trial court level, witnesses testify, exhibits are introduced, and the attorneys argue the case. Once the case is concluded, either the court or the jury decides what the facts are and applies the law to the facts. The losing side may appeal the decision to a higher court.

> In 1994, the following numbers of cases were filed in U.S. trial courts:
>
> • Civil: 18 million
> • Criminal: 13 million
> • Traffic: 50 million
> • Juvenile: 1.8 million.
>
> **Source:** State Court Caseload Statistics (1994), National Center for State Courts

A fairly recent phenomenon is the presence of television cameras in the courtroom. In the interest of public education, an open society, and the "right to know," some courts have opened their doors to the public and allowed the proceedings to be broadcast on TV. It's a judge's decision on a case-by-case basis whether to allow media coverage. Adoption, dependency, and mental health cases are usually closed hearings.

Each level of court has its own judges and its own qualifications to become a judge. You don't necessarily have to be a lawyer to become a judge. Depending on where you live, you'll either have to run for office or seek to be appointed. Generally, a higher degree of education is required for judges in courts responsible for higher-dollar lawsuits. Many judgeships require a minimum of law school, state bar admission to practice, and three to five years of legal practice.

"What is a jury?"

A jury has been described as a random slice of the community chosen to decide a lawsuit. After you turn eighteen, you may receive a notice in the mail requiring you to appear for jury duty at any of the nation's courts where trials take place. Your name is randomly selected from different sources, such as the motor vehicle or voter registration lists.

The process of a jury weighing the evidence and deciding the facts of a case began in Europe in the 1700s. Juries decide the facts of a case by considering the evidence presented by both sides. The evidence may be *physical* (a gun, X-rays), *demonstrative* (charts or diagrams), and *testimonial* (witnesses who take the stand and testify). Once the jury determines what happened, its only duty is to apply the law to those facts. The judge tells the jury what the laws are regarding the case. A verdict is reached by applying the law to the facts of the case.

You may be one of six to twelve members sworn in to decide a civil or criminal case. If you have a good reason not to serve, you may be excused. For example, the nature of your work or a family emergency may keep you from serving. If you're excused, you may be called for jury duty at a later date. The length of the trial is also taken into consideration.

In choosing a jury, any form of discrimination is prohibited. You can't be excluded solely because of your race, gender, religion, or ethnicity. Once you're called to the courthouse as part of a pool to be interviewed, you may be excused for various reasons, but not if purely discriminatory. Only prison inmates and the mentally ill are excused as a class from jury duty. Even George Bush, Jr., the governor of Texas, and Rudolph Guiliani, the mayor of New York City, were called for jury duty in 1996.

You may be paid a fee for each day you serve, as well as travel expenses. These vary around the country. Depending on the type of case, you may be *sequestered* during all or part of the trial. The purpose of sequestering is to protect or insulate you from outside influences. Once sequestered, the jury stays together until it reaches a verdict. The court makes arrangements for your meals

- About 45% of Americans who are sent jury notices show up at the courthouse. (Some notices aren't received, and some are ignored. Some people get excused before their date of appearance.)
- Of those who appear, almost two-thirds avoid serving on juries due to work, personal conflicts, illness, or a lawyer's challenge.

Source: Study by National Center for State Courts, quoted in *The Jury: Disorder in the Court* by Stephen J. Adler (Doubleday, 1994)

and overnights in a hotel. The court bailiff is your contact with the outside world and is responsible for seeing that your needs are met. There may be restrictions on which newspapers, magazines, and TV or radio programs are available to you while you're sequestered. Because sequestering is expensive and inconvenient to jurors and their families, it's rare to sequester a jury.

You may have a teen court in your community. This is a peer review program that allows middle school and high school students the opportunity to participate in a fellow student's case. With the guidance of local attorneys and a judge, you and your friends can decide the penalty for unlawful behavior. This usually applies to misdemeanors and petty offenses only, not felonies.

> A number of states allow jury trials in juvenile court, including Alaska, Colorado, Kansas, Massachusetts, Michigan, Montana, New Mexico, Oklahoma, Texas, West Virginia, Wisconsin, and Wyoming.

In most states, there are no juries in juvenile court because the Constitution doesn't require it. The juvenile court judge acts as both the jury (in deciding the facts) and the judge (in applying the law to the facts). If a juvenile is transferred to adult court, a jury may be used to decide the case.

Here are a few other jury terms you may be wondering about:

- *Foreman.* The man or woman designated to speak for the jury, selected by the jury at the beginning of their deliberations.
- *Deliberation.* Once the formal presentation of evidence during the trial ends, the case is turned over to the jury. Their duty is to decide the facts of the case, apply the law given to them by the judge, and reach a decision. To *deliberate,* as applied to a jury, means to consider and weigh the facts as a group.
- *Instructions.* These are the laws about the subject matter of the case (such as what negligence is in a car accident case or what the legal definition of shoplifting is). The instructions are stated to the jury by the judge. Some courts allow the jury to keep a copy of the instructions during deliberations.

- *Verdict.* The formal finding or decision of the jury. It's decided in secret, with only the jury members present, and then reported to the court.
- *Hung jury.* This means the jury is deadlocked or unable to reach a verdict after a reasonable time of deliberation. This results in a *mistrial,* where the case may be retried or possibly settled by the parties without a trial.
- *Jury view.* A jury is taken to an accident scene to view where the event took place. For example, the jury in the O.J. Simpson criminal trial was taken to both the defendant's home and the scene of the crime. Jury views are rare.
- *Grand jury.* A group of twelve to twenty-three men and women who are sworn in to consider evidence presented to them by the prosecutor. Their job is to determine whether there's a reason to believe *(probable cause)* that a crime has been committed and who committed it. The grand jury doesn't determine guilt or innocence. In deciding that a crime has been committed, the grand jury votes for charging the person responsible, which results in an *indictment.* The person charged either pleads guilty or not guilty. If not guilty, he or she may go to trial before a regular jury of six to twelve people.

FYI

Rent a movie and learn more about our legal system. Here are eight classic films that offer insights into the roles of jurors, judges, and lawyers:

- *Anatomy of a Murder* (1959). The story of a murder trial in rural Michigan.
- *Bananas* (1971). A classic Woody Allen movie; he represents himself at trial, and he also cross-examines himself.
- *The Caine Mutiny* (1954). This action film about World War II in the Pacific includes a fictional court-martial of a naval officer.
- *Criminal Justice* (1990). A look at the criminal justice system from knife assault to verdict. (NOTE: This movie is rated R for language and violence.)

- *Gideon's Trumpet* (1980). An account of the U.S. Supreme Court decision that granted poor criminal defendants a right to counsel. It depicts criminal justice at its worst and best.
- *The Ox-Bow Incident* (1943). The trial of an accused horse thief by other cowboys gives a chilling view of frontier justice.
- *To Kill a Mockingbird* (1962). A rape prosecution in a small town in the Deep South.
- *Twelve Angry Men* (1957). Jury deliberations in a murder trial.

"Is every court decision final?"

Once a decision is made by a judge or a jury at the trial court level, anyone can ask a higher court to review his or her case. The right to appeal isn't automatic in every case. You need to check your state's rules about the appeal process. Also check the time requirements and deadlines so you don't miss one.

At the appellate court level, none of the excitement or drama of a trial occurs. The job of a court of appeals or your state's highest court is to review what took place during the trial and determine whether any mistakes were made.

There are no juries or testimony by witnesses involved in an appeal. An appeal focuses on written arguments, called *briefs,* about the issues raised by the lawyers on each side of the case. Sometimes the appellate court allows the attorneys to orally argue their position—which also gives the court the opportunity to question the attorneys about certain points of law or facts of the case.

There's no such thing as a perfect trial. Mistakes are made by the attorneys, witnesses, and the court. The appellate court looks at the errors pointed out by the attorneys in their briefs, and decides whether they are serious enough to merit action. If what took place at trial amounts to what's referred to as *harmless error,* the decision will remain. If, however, *fundamental error* occurred affecting the defendant's rights, the trial court decision may be reversed or modified.

If you suffer a loss in the case because of an attorney's error or negligence, you may consider a malpractice lawsuit against the attorney. There's a difference between gross error or negligence and an attorney's theory of a case and trial strategy. Judges have immunity from such a lawsuit, even if what they did was clearly wrong. In order for judges to competently "judge" the many matters before them without fear of being sued, the law grants them protection. This is limited to official court business and doesn't cover unrelated acts in the judge's private life.

In a criminal case, a reversal may mean a new trial for the accused. In a civil case, it may also mean a new trial or a settlement of the case, as opposed to the time and expense of a new trial. If you had a free lawyer representing you at trial, he or she may be appointed to continue representing you on appeal.

Generally, in criminal or delinquency cases, teenagers are appointed a lawyer (public defender). This is also true in abuse, neglect, and abandonment cases. In other types of cases, free legal representation may not be available. However, through community legal services or similar legal clinics, advice and/or assistance on a sliding scale fee may be available.

Community Legal Services (Legal Aid) is a federally funded program that provides free assistance to low-income individuals. To qualify, a family of one can't earn more than $9,600 a year; for a family of four, the limit is $19,500. Legal aid attorneys handle domestic relations and domestic violence cases, as well as issues regarding housing, homelessness, migrant children, education, bankruptcy, consumer rights, and health-related matters. Generally, representation isn't available for criminal, abortion, or immigration matters.

Oral arguments in appellate courts are open to the public. See if you can arrange for your civics or social studies class to attend one. Write or call the court in advance and find out what cases are scheduled. Then your class may select one of particular interest to sit in on.

"What happens in juvenile court?"

Some people may call it "juvy," "children's court," "juvenile court," or "juvenile hall." The names change from state to state, but the court's job and authority over you are the same. Your age determines whether you'll appear in juvenile or adult court. In most states, juvenile court jurisdiction ends at age eighteen. In a few states, you may remain under the authority of the juvenile court until you're twenty-one.

Juvenile courts deal with children and teenagers in cases involving child abuse and neglect, abandonment by parents, termination of parents' rights, and adoption. All delinquency and incorrigibility* cases are handled in juvenile court. Miscellaneous hearings covering name changes, mental health issues, and abortion may be conducted in the juvenile court.

Once you're involved with the juvenile court, you have many of the same rights as an adult. You may be appointed an attorney to represent you or a guardian to speak about what's in your best interests.

In a delinquency case (where you're charged with breaking the law), you may remain silent, plead guilty or not guilty, and go to trial if you choose. In some states, you may be entitled to a jury trial. You may also have the right to appeal a decision that you disagree with.

The trials or hearings in juvenile court aren't as formal as those in adult court or the cases you see on TV. The philosophy of juvenile justice is treatment and rehabilitation, not punishment, although the pendulum is beginning to swing toward greater consequences. If you're not locked up for a period of time or sent to the department of corrections, you may be placed on probation, which could last until you turn eighteen or twenty-one. You may be released early if you follow all the terms of your probation and you don't break any more laws. Your probation officer meets with you on a regular basis and stays in touch with your

During 1992:

- 533,000 juveniles were placed on probation.
- 296,000 spent time in detention (47% for property crimes).
- 121,000 delinquents were placed out of home—in training schools, camps, residential treatment facilities, or group homes.

Source: *Juvenile Offenders and Victims: A National Report,* National Center for Juvenile Justice (1995)

---

* See Chapter 7, pages 140–141.

parents and teachers. If you violate your probation, you'll find yourself back in court facing more serious consequences.

A fairly new aspect of rehabilitation is juvenile boot camp, or what some states call "shock incarceration." It's designed for older juvenile offenders (fifteen to seventeen years) and is used as a last resort. Boot camp often takes several months and is highly structured; juveniles are subject to firm discipline and strenuous exercise. Upon completion, there's a second phase of rehabilitation, with less supervision and greater freedom. The goal is to eventually release the offenders from all court and probation supervision, with little risk to the community.

In the noncriminal cases in juvenile court (abuse, neglect, and adoption), you may be involved as a witness. These are considered civil cases, meaning that you won't receive any time in detention or with the department of corrections. You may be placed by the court in a foster home or residential treatment center until the problems that brought you to the court's attention are worked out.

"What if I'm tried in adult court?"

Regardless of your age, if your crime is serious, the prosecutor may file charges against you in adult court or ask the juvenile court to transfer you to adult court. All states have a procedure that allows juveniles to be tried as adults. Some states have adopted an automatic transfer rule, which means you go directly to adult court for certain crimes.

Drastic changes in the juvenile justice system have occurred in the past few years. Due to an epidemic of juvenile crime, a get-tough attitude has swept the United States. Most states have changed their laws to put more teenagers in the adult system. The philosophy of treatment and rehabilitation is giving way to longer sentences and fewer services for minors.

- Between 1989 and 1993, 11,800 juveniles were transferred to adult courts.
- 96% of juveniles transferred were males.
- 12% were age 15 or younger.

Source: *Juvenile Offenders and Victims: A National Report,* National Center for Juvenile Justice (1995), with 1996 *Update on Violence*

Sixteen-year-old Morris Kent was on probation when he was charged with rape and robbery. He confessed to the charges and was transferred to adult court. No investigation was done before the transfer, and the court didn't state the reasons for sending Morris to the adult system. He was found guilty and sentenced to thirty to ninety years in prison. The U.S. Supreme Court reversed the transfer, stating that Morris, although a juvenile, was entitled to full due process—which meant a hearing, investigation, and a written statement of the court's decision and reasons.

Since Morris's case, any juvenile charged with a crime, with a possibility of transfer to adult court, is entitled to full due process. A lawyer is appointed to represent you. It's the prosecutor's job to present evidence to the court regarding the seriousness of the charge and why you should be tried as an adult rather than a juvenile. Your lawyer will argue in favor of you staying in the juvenile system for treatment and rehabilitation.

The court must determine not only what's best *for* you but also how to protect the community *from* you until rehabilitation occurs. Community safety is a priority. Some of the factors the court considers include your age and level of maturity, the time remaining to work with you in the juvenile system, the seriousness of the crime, your criminal history, family support, and whether services have been offered to you in the past.

If you're not transferred to adult court, your case will proceed as a juvenile court matter, where jurisdiction ends at age eighteen or twenty-one. If you're transferred to adult court, you'll be afforded all the rights of an adult criminal defendant. This also means that the penalties usually reserved for adults now apply to you—including a number of years in prison, and in some cases, a life sentence or the death penalty.

"Can I be put in jail?"

Yes. If you're locked up, against your will and away from your home, you're in jail. It may be referred to as *detention, lock-up, secure care,* or some other less harsh term than jail, but your freedom is still restricted.

At the point you first become involved with the police, you may experience a stay in detention. If you're arrested, you can be taken into custody and held for approximately forty-eight hours. If formal charges aren't filed within that period, you'll be released. If charges are filed, you'll appear in court within a day or two, and the judge will decide if you'll be detained further or released to a responsible person.

If you're a danger to yourself or others, you may be held until the next hearing. This could be several weeks. If you're found not guilty, you'll be released. If you're found guilty by the court or you plead guilty, you may be detained until sentencing takes place. At that point, you may receive additional time in a locked facility. Or you may be placed on probation with a designated number of days in detention.

- There are over 60,000 teenagers (mostly boys) in custody in the juvenile system.
- The average jail stay is 1 year for crimes against persons, 248 days for drug offenses, and 187 days for weapons offenses.

Source: *Juvenile Offenders and Victims: A National Report,* National Center for Juvenile Justice (1995)

There are any number of opportunities to lock you up once you're in the juvenile system. If you're placed on probation and you violate your terms, you're sure to spend time in detention. If you're sent to the corrections department, you could remain there until you're eighteen, until you complete your sentence, or until the department releases you on parole. States differ on the length of stay for juveniles in locked facilities.

Teenagers determined by the court to be incorrigible* may also be locked up. This often happens with teenagers who are chronic runaways or who are out of control at home. Courts are reluctant to release teens knowing they'll be on the streets that night.

In some states, the law requires that detained teens be kept separate from adult prisoners. Many facilities around the country

---

* See Chapter 7, pages 140–141.

are separate buildings where no contact with adults is possible. Teenagers who are tried as adults and sentenced to jail or prison may also be kept separate until they turn eighteen. Then they join the general adult prison population. A scary thought!

"Does the death penalty apply to me?"

When Billy was fifteen years old, he and his brother and two friends brutally murdered Billy's brother-in-law. Billy kicked and shot the victim in the head, slit his throat, and dragged his body, chained to a concrete block, to a river, where it remained for almost four weeks.

Billy was transferred to adult court, tried by a jury, and sentenced to death for first-degree murder. Billy appealed his case, which was eventually heard by the U.S. Supreme Court. In 1988, the court issued its decision, which remains the law today regarding juveniles and the death penalty.

The court stated that the execution of any person under sixteen at the time of his or her offense would offend civilized standards of decency: "[M]inors often lack the experience, perspective, and judgment expected of adults. . . . The normal fifteen-year-old is not prepared to assume the full responsibilities of an adult." Billy's death sentence was set aside, and he was resentenced.

Eleven states and the District of Columbia ban capital punishment altogether. In thirteen states, the death penalty is banned for persons who were juveniles at the time of committing the crime. This means that in the remaining twenty-six states, a teenager who's sixteen or older at the time of the offense may be given the death penalty.

Most juveniles on death row in the United States are there because of a homicide. From 1980

- Between 1900 and 1950, approximately 20 teenagers under 16 were executed. Before 1900, two 10-year-olds were executed, as well as one 11-year-old and five 12-year-olds.
- The United States is one of only 6 countries that has executed a juvenile (under 18) since 1990. The other countries include Nigeria, Pakistan, Iran, Iraq, and Saudi Arabia.

Sources: Victor L. Streib, *Death Penalty for Juveniles* (Indiana University Press, 1987); Sherri Jackson, "Too Young to Die: Juveniles and the Death Penalty," *New England Journal on Criminal and Civil Confinement,* Spring 1996

through 1994, juveniles killed 27,000 victims—over 2,300 in 1994 alone. Since 1980, as many as thirty-five juvenile homicide offenders each year are younger than twelve. The U.S. has witnessed a 94 percent increase in juvenile homicides since 1984.

Death Penalty for Juveniles by Victor L. Streib (Indiana University Press, 1987).

Teens and the Death Penalty by Elaine Landau (Enslow Publishers, 1992). Discusses the specific relation of capital punishment to juvenile offenders, provides a historical overview of the establishment of the death penalty in the U.S., discusses reasons people favor or oppose it, and describes methods of execution.

"Can my juvenile record be destroyed?"

Adults of all ages return to court asking for their juvenile records to be destroyed. The reasons vary: a new job, continuing education, a credit application, or military service. You don't necessarily have to have a specific reason. You may just want to clear the record, since what you did as a youth shouldn't adversely affect the rest of your life.

Having a record means that your name, charge, and other vital statistics have been entered into a local and/or national computer system. Once you're charged with a crime or delinquent act and found guilty, you have a record. In some jurisdictions, the fact that you were arrested, whether convicted of a charge or not, may result in a record. So it's worth knowing in advance what the law is in your state.

Most states have a procedure whereby juvenile records may be destroyed. The decision is usually *discretionary*—destruction isn't automatic upon request. You may be required to appear in court to discuss your request with the judge. In most situations, it's not necessary to have a lawyer.

The court will want to know why you want your record destroyed. They'll ask what you're doing now (school, job, family, etc.), and whether you've had any problems with the law since becoming an adult. If you can show the court that you've been rehabilitated, your request will be granted. On the other hand, if you continue to have brushes with the law, are on probation as an adult, or have outstanding traffic tickets, your request may be denied. You can always renew your request at a later date, when a period of time has passed without incident.

The court also takes into consideration what your juvenile offenses were, your age at the time of the offenses, and whether you've successfully completed your consequences. If you still owe work hours or restitution, for example, it's unlikely that your juvenile record will be destroyed. Make sure you come to court in the best possible position.

A twenty-two-year-old once asked a court to destroy his juvenile record, including a number of burglaries and shoplifting charges. When asked why, he stated that he was scheduled to be sentenced the following week in adult court for armed robbery. He didn't want the judge to know about his juvenile history, which would justify a harsher penalty. Do you think the judge had to think long and hard about this request?

FYI 🌍

Find out more about the legal system and the law on these Web sites created especially for teenagers:

LAWKids' Only!
http://wwlia.org/kidsonly.htm
A fun and fascinating part of the extensive World Wide Legal Information Association (WWLIA) site. Includes a Timetable of World Legal history, information on the history of Canadian law, and links to a legal dictionary, "Police Station," tongue-in-cheek "Law School," lawyer jokes, and a list of the dumbest things ever said in court.

Legal Pad Junior for Teens
http://www.legalpadjr.com/teens.htm
Includes message pads, chats, clubs, a "2B Heard" newsletter by and for teens, online legal help, and more.

Teen Court TV
http://www.courttv.com/teens/
An educational site with court cases of interest to teens.

Think About It, Talk About It

1. A four-year-old girl sleeping on her livingroom couch was shot and killed by a stray bullet in a drive-by shooting. A sixteen-year-old boy was arrested and transferred to adult court for murder. You're eighteen and have been called to serve on the jury. The prosecutor is going to ask for the death penalty if the defendant is found guilty.

What do you think about this case? Could you be an impartial juror? If asked, could you vote for the death penalty? What do you think about teens serving on juries where other teenagers are on trial?

2. Bobby is seventeen years, eleven months old. The juvenile court in Bobby's state has jurisdiction over minors until they turn eighteen. Bobby has a clean record, goes to school, and works part-time. Just before his eighteenth birthday, he's caught transporting sixty pounds of marijuana. He was going to be paid $500 cash to take a suitcase to the airport and check it on a certain flight. But an airport drug-sniffing dog caught him in the act. Because of the amount of marijuana, he was charged with possession for sale and transportation. The state wants him transferred to adult court.

What do you think? With only one month remaining before Bobby turns eighteen, is there time for rehabilitation? Does the quantity of drugs make the crime more serious? If he's not transferred and instead is handled in the juvenile system for one month, isn't that just a slap on the wrist? What kind of message should be sent in this case?

3. A six-year-old California boy kicked and beat a four-week-old. The baby suffered two skull fractures, brain damage, and internal bleeding. The boy was originally charged with attempted murder and burglary, which was later changed to assault.

What should be done for and with this child? Should he be tried as an adult because of the seriousness of his acts? Should he be tried at all?

4. A new law in Illinois permits children as young as ten to be sent to prison. In 1994, two Chicago boys, ages ten and eleven, dangled five-year-old Eric out of a fifteenth floor apartment window for not stealing candy for them. Eric's eight-year-old brother tried to rescue him, but Eric fell to his death. In 1996, the two boys, then twelve and thirteen, were sent to the state's juvenile penitentiary, making them the nation's youngest inmates at a high-security prison.

What do you think about prison for young offenders? How long should they stay? Should they receive counseling, schooling, and/or special treatment?

Appendix

Availability of Adoption Records

How old do you have to be to request and obtain adoption records? That depends on the state in which the adoption took place. In some states, adoption records are *sealed,* meaning that no information is available. Some states will release *nonidentifying* information, meaning that they won't provide the names of your birth parents but will provide other information about them. This may require their consent or the consent of the court. Some states will release *identifying* information, including names, once you turn eighteen. And some states have a *confidential intermediary* program that assists in providing adoption information and locating persons involved in adoptions. Check with your local court for information about this program.

> **NOTE:** Adoption law is changing. Before taking any action, check with a librarian or adoption lawyer in your state. For more specific information about records availability in Canada, check with a librarian or adoption lawyer in your province.

State or Province	Nonidentifying Information	Identifying Information	Confidential Intermediary
Alabama	19	—	yes
Alaska	18	—	—
Arizona	18	21	yes
Arkansas	18	21	—
California	18–21	—	—
Colorado	21	—	yes
Connecticut	18	18	yes
Delaware	sealed	—	—
District of Columbia	sealed	—	—
Florida	21	—	yes

Continued

State or Province	Nonidentifying Information	Identifying Information	Confidential Intermediary
Georgia	21	—	yes ·
Hawaii	18	18	yes
Idaho	sealed	—	—
Illinois	18	—	yes
Indiana	21	21	—
Iowa	sealed	18	—
Kansas	18	18	—
Kentucky	18	21	yes
Louisiana	sealed	—	yes
Maine	18 (with court's consent)	—	—
Maryland	18	—	—
Massachusetts	18	18	—
Michigan	18	18	yes
Minnesota	18	18	yes
Mississippi	sealed	—	—
Missouri	21	21	yes
Montana	sealed	—	yes
Nebraska	25	25	yes
Nevada	sealed	—	—
New Hampshire	21	21	—
New Jersey	18	—	—
New Mexico	18	18	—
New York	18 (through a confidential intermediary)	—	yes
North Carolina	18	—	—
North Dakota	sealed	18	—
Ohio	sealed	—	yes
Oklahoma	sealed	—	—
Oregon	18	—	yes
Pennsylvania	18	18	yes
Rhode Island	21	—	—
South Carolina	18	18	—
South Dakota	18	18	—
Tennessee	18	21	yes

Continued

State or Province	Nonidentifying Information	Identifying Information	Confidential Intermediary
Texas	21	—	—
Utah	sealed	—	—
Vermont	21 (with consents of birth parents)	—	—
Virginia	18 (with consents of birth parents)	—	—
Washington	21	21	yes
West Virginia	18	—	—
Wisconsin	18	—	yes
Wyoming	—	—	yes
CANADA			
British Columbia	yes	—	—
Manitoba	yes	—	—
New Brunswick	yes	—	—
Newfoundland	yes	—	—
Northwest Territories	yes	—	—
Nova Scotia	yes	—	—
Ontario	yes	—	—
Quebec	14	—	—
Saskatchewan	yes	—	—
Yukon	yes (with consents)	—	—

Source: *The Adoption Directory*, 2d ed., by Ellen Paul (Detroit: Gale Research, Inc., 1995).

Custody Factors

If your parents get a divorce, will the court listen to your wishes about who will get custody of you and how the custody arrangements will work? Will the court appoint an attorney or guardian to advocate for you? That depends on which state you live in. Here's a state-by-state chart that answers these questions. An "X" means yes.

State	Children's Wishes	Attorney or Guardian Appointed
Alabama	—	—
Alaska	X	X
Arizona	X	X
Arkansas	—	—
California	X	X
Colorado	X	X
Connecticut	X	X
Delaware	X	X
District of Columbia	X	X
Florida	X	X
Georgia	X	X
Hawaii	X	X
Idaho	X	—
Illinois	X	X
Indiana	X	X
Iowa	X	X
Kansas	X	—
Kentucky	X	X
Louisiana	X	—
Maine	X	X
Maryland	—	X
Massachusetts	—	X
Michigan	X	X
Minnesota	X	X
Mississippi	—	—
Missouri	X	X
Montana	X	X

Continued

State	Children's Wishes	Attorney or Guardian Appointed
Nebraska	X	X
Nevada	X	X
New Hampshire	X	X
New Jersey	X	X
New Mexico	X	X
New York	X	X
North Carolina	X	—
North Dakota	X	X
Ohio	X	X
Oklahoma	X	—
Oregon	X	X
Pennsylvania	—	X
Rhode Island	X	X
South Carolina	X	X
South Dakota	X	X
Tennessee	X	X
Texas	X	X
Utah	X	X
Vermont	—	X
Virginia	X	X
Washington	X	X
West Virginia	X	—
Wisconsin	X	X
Wyoming	X	—
CANADA	X	X

Compulsory School Attendance

At what ages do you have to go to school? Here's a state-by-state chart showing the ages of compulsory school attendance. If you have questions about exceptions or specific requirements, check the laws in your state or province.

State	Ages of Compulsory School Attendance	State	Ages of Compulsory School Attendance
Alabama	7–16	Nebraska	7–16
Alaska	7–16	Nevada	7–17
Arizona	6–16	New Hampshire	6–16
Arkansas	5–17	New Jersey	6–16
California	6–18	New Mexico	5–16
Colorado	7–16	New York	6–16
Connecticut	7–16	North Carolina	7–16
Delaware	5–16	North Dakota	7–16
District of Columbia	7–17	Ohio	6–18
Florida	6–16	Oklahoma	5–18
Georgia	7–16	Oregon	7–18
Hawaii	6–18	Pennsylvania	8–17
Idaho	7–16	Rhode Island	6–16
Illinois	7–16	South Carolina	5–17
Indiana	7–16	South Dakota	6–16
Iowa	6–16	Tennessee	7–17
Kansas	7–16	Texas	6–17
Kentucky	6–16	Utah	6–18
Louisiana	7–17	Vermont	7–16
Maine	7–17	Virginia	5–18
Maryland	5–16	Washington	8–18
Massachusetts	6–16	West Virginia	6–16
Michigan	6–16	Wisconsin	6–18
Minnesota	7–16	Wyoming	7–16
Mississippi	6–16		
Missouri	7–16	**CANADA**	6–16
Montana	7–16		

Corporal Punishment in Schools

Does the law in your state ban corporal punishment in schools? Check this chart to find out.

NOTE: A Yes followed by an asterisk (Yes*) means that state law bans corporal punishment in the schools but allows reasonable force to be used to maintain safety and order, for self-defense, or to protect other students.

State	Does state law ban corporal punishment in public schools?	State	Does state law ban corporal punishment in public schools?
Alabama	No	Nebraska	Yes
Alaska	No	Nevada	Yes*
Arizona	No	New Hampshire	No
Arkansas	No	New Jersey	Yes*
California	Yes	New Mexico	No
Colorado	No	New York	No
Connecticut	Yes*	North Carolina	No
Delaware	No	North Dakota	Yes*
District of Columbia	No	Ohio	No
Florida	No	Oklahoma	No
Georgia	No	Oregon	Yes*
Hawaii	Yes	Pennsylvania	No
Idaho	No	Rhode Island	No
Illinois	Yes*	South Carolina	No
Indiana	No	South Dakota	No
Iowa	Yes*	Tennessee	No
Kansas	No	Texas	No
Kentucky	No	Utah	No
Louisiana	No	Vermont	Yes*
Maine	Yes	Virginia	Yes*
Maryland	Yes	Washington	Yes
Massachusetts	Yes	West Virginia	Yes
Michigan	Yes*	Wisconsin	Yes*
Minnesota	Yes*	Wyoming	No
Mississippi	No		
Missouri	No	**CANADA**	No
Montana	Yes*		

Compulsory Provision of Services for Special Education

All states are required to provide special education services for students who qualify for them. If you're between the ages listed for your state, and if you're in need of special education services, you're entitled to receive them from your school district. Be sure to check your state's laws for exceptions or specific requirements.

State	Ages of Compulsory Provision of Services for Special Education	State	Ages of Compulsory Provision of Services for Special Education
Alabama	3–20	Montana	3–18
Alaska	3–21	Nebraska	Birth–20
Arizona	3–21	Nevada	3–21
Arkansas	3–20	New Hampshire	3–20
California	3–21	New Jersey	3–21
Colorado	3–20	New Mexico	3–21
Connecticut	3–21	New York	3–21
Delaware	3–20	North Carolina	3–20
District of Columbia	3–21	North Dakota	3–20
Florida	3–18	Ohio	3–21
Georgia	3–21	Oklahoma	3–21
Hawaii	3–20	Oregon	3–20
Idaho	3–20	Pennsylvania	3–21
Illinois	3–20	Rhode Island	3–20
Indiana	3–17	South Carolina	3–20
Iowa	Birth–20	South Dakota	3–20
Kansas	3–21	Tennessee	3–21
Kentucky	3–20	Texas	3–21
Louisiana	3–21	Utah	3–21
Maine	3–19	Vermont	3–21
Maryland	Birth–20	Virginia	2–21
Massachusetts	3–21	Washington	3–21
Michigan	Birth–25	West Virginia	3–22
Minnesota	Birth–20	Wisconsin	3–20
Mississippi	3–20	Wyoming	3–20
Missouri	3–20		

Glossary

Adoptive home study. An investigation and report, usually by a social worker, of a single person or couple wishing to adopt a child. The study covers all aspects of the applicant's life including motivation to adopt; medical, criminal and social history; education and career; finances; marriages; and a fingerprint check. It also includes statements from relatives and references from nonrelatives.

Age of majority. In most states, 18 is recognized as the age of adulthood, entitling you to make your own decisions and manage your personal affairs.

AIDS. Stands for *Acquired Immunodeficiency Syndrome,* a breakdown of the body's defense system caused by HIV, which kills blood cells. Research continues for a cure. In the meantime, be aware of the dangers of unprotected sex and drug use (needles).

Alternate Dispute Resolution (ADR). A method of settling a disagreement without going to court. It's intended to save time, money, and aggravation. Two types of ADR are *arbitration* and *mediation.*

Appeal. The right to ask a higher court (called an *appellate court*) to review a decision made by a lower court. This is done by reading a transcript of what took place in the lower court, and listening to the oral arguments of the attorneys involved. The attorneys may also file written arguments about their case called *briefs.*

Arbitration. A process in which both sides of a dispute agree to allow a third person (who is not involved) to settle their differences. You may choose the arbitrator yourself, or one will be chosen for you. The arbitrator's decision is binding on both sides.

Beneficiary. Someone who receives something; often used to describe the person named in a will or a life insurance policy.

Brief. A concise, written statement about a case, with arguments about issues raised by the lawyers. Briefs are read by the appellate court and help in making decisions about these issues.

Capital punishment. The death penalty.

Censorship. The act of limiting access to material found objectionable; for example, books, movies, and music with explicit sexual content, violence, or profanity.

Child Protective Services (CPS). A government agency responsible for investigating reports of child abuse, neglect, and abandonment. A CPS caseworker may remove children from the home and is required to offer services to reunite the family.

Conscientious objector. A person who refuses to serve in the military or bear arms because of his or her moral or religious beliefs.

Corporal punishment. Physical discipline including swats, paddling, and spanking.

Custodial interference. Violation of or interference with a lawful custody order of the court, by the noncustodial parent or anyone else.

Deadbeat Dad. A father who is ordered by a court to pay child support and fails to pay. (This may apply to mothers as well.)

Delinquent. A minor who violates a criminal law. If found guilty, he or she is called a *juvenile delinquent.*

Detention. Temporary confinement of a minor in a locked facility. This may be as a consequence of an action committed by the minor, or for the safety of the minor or the community between hearings.

Disaffirm. To get out of a contract without meeting all of its terms.

Discrimination. The act of treating an individual or a group differently than others because of race, gender, religion, nationality or disability. Not all discrimination is illegal. Teenagers have age restrictions regarding employment, curfew, alcohol, and driving, all of which are legal.

Double jeopardy. Going to trial a second time for the same offense. There are exceptions to this, but generally you're protected against the government trying you twice.

Due process. Also called *due process of law,* this is your right to enforce and protect your individual rights (life, liberty, and property) through notice of any action against you, and the right to be heard and confront the opposing side.

Emancipation. The process of becoming legally free from your parents or guardian. This may be the result of a court order, an act on your part (marriage, enlistment), or other circumstances your state's laws allow. If you're emancipated, your parents lose their authority over you and are no longer responsible for you.

Felony. A classification of the criminal laws which carries the strictest penalties, usually a minimum of one year in jail. A felony is more serious than a misdemeanor or petty offense.

Foster care. When a child is removed from his or her home by Child Protective Services (CPS), the police, or by court order, he or she is placed in a home until safe to return to the parents. Placement may be in a foster home, child crisis center, group home, or emergency receiving home. These homes are usually licensed and regulated by the government.

Guardian. An individual with the lawful power and duty to take care of another person, including his or her property and financial affairs. The court may appoint a guardian for a minor if necessary, and sometimes the minor may select a guardian or object to the one being considered. A guardian may also be selected by your parents and named in their will.

HIV. Stands for the *Human Immunodeficiency Virus,* which causes AIDS. The body's immune system is made up of white blood cells (T-cells) which protect us from infection. The virus kills the T-cells, lowering the body's defenses against disease and infection.

Incorrigible child. A child (usually a teenager) who breaks rules or laws that don't apply to adults. Examples include missing school, running away, using alcohol or tobacco, and disobeying parents or guardians.

Intestate. If you die without a will, you are intestate. Your possessions will go to whomever your state law names. Most likely, they will remain in the family, because the law states that they go to your parents, brothers, and sisters.

Jurisdiction. The legal right of a judge and a court to exercise its authority; the power to hear and determine a case. Specific rules exist regarding jurisdiction. Without it, a court is powerless to act.

Mediation. A way of settling a dispute which includes a third person, who is neutral and attempts to get both sides to reach an agreement. Mediation is used in family and juvenile court.

Minor. Someone who is not yet legally an adult.

Miranda warnings. These are the rights suspects are read when in police custody. You have the right to remain silent; to have a lawyer appointed to represent you; if you cannot afford a lawyer, one will be appointed for you; and any statement you make may be used against you in a court of law. As a result of the *Gault* decision (see Chapter 6, pages 133 and 135), these rights belong to minors as well as adults.

Misdemeanor. A criminal offense less serious than a felony, with a jail sentence of one year or less.

Petty offense. A crime with a maximum penalty of (usually) a few months in jail or a fine. No prison time is given, and the fines are often set by law up to several hundred dollars.

Power of attorney. A written document giving someone else the authority to act for you—to obtain medical care, for example, in the absence of your parents. See Chapter 6, page 134, for a sample form.

Probation. A program in which you're supervised by the court or probation department for a period of time. Special terms of probation may include time in detention, community service hours, counseling, a fine, or restitution.

Restitution. The act of restoring a victim to the position the victim was in before suffering property damage or loss or personal injury. A minor placed on probation may be required to pay the victim back for any loss that the minor caused. If the amount is great, payment may be spread out over months or years.

Search and seizure. The ability of a person in a position of authority (police or school teacher) to search you or your property (room, car, locker) and take anything unlawful or not legally in your possession.

Self-incrimination. Since you have the right to remain silent (see *Miranda warnings* above), you aren't required to help the police build their case against you. You don't have to be a witness against yourself. This protection comes from the Fifth Amendment of the U.S. Constitution.

Sequester. To sequester a jury means to isolate them or separate them from their families and the public until the case is decided. This is rarely done, and usually only in high-profile or sensational trials.

Sexually transmitted disease (STD). A disease contracted as a result of sexual activity. STDs require immediate medical treatment.

Shared custody. When the court gives both parents in a divorce the responsibility to share the care and control of their children. Sometimes called *joint custody.*

Sole custody. When one parent in a divorce receives custody of the child, and the other parent is given liberal visitation rights (for example, weekends, vacations, and summer).

Statutory rape. Unlawful sexual relations with a person under the age of consent, which may be 16, 17, or 18, depending on your state. It's a crime even if the underage person consents.

Termination of parental rights. A legal process by which the relationship between a child and his or her parents is ended. The biological parents are no longer the legal parents of the child, which frees the child for adoption. Some reasons for terminating a parent's rights include abuse or neglect of the child, abandonment, mental illness or criminal history of the parent, or severe alcohol or drug use.

Testate. If you die with a will, you are testate. Your wishes as stated in your will are followed unless they're illegal or against public policy.

Transfer. In juvenile law, this is the process by which a minor is charged with a crime and tried in adult court rather than juvenile court. Due to the seriousness of the charge and the juvenile's history, he or she may be treated as an adult, making the juvenile eligible for adult consequences including life imprisonment or the death penalty.

Truancy. The failure to go to school when required unless you're excused by the school for a good reason, such as illness, a doctor's appointment, or a family emergency. In some states, truancy is an offense that could land you in court.

Will. A written document describing how you want your possessions distributed when you die. In most states, you must be 18 years old to make a will, but you may be any age to be a beneficiary and receive something from someone else's will. See Chapter 1, page 25, for a sample form.

Worker's compensation. A program for employees that covers your expenses for work-related injuries or illness. It's a no-fault program, which means that you're paid even if the accident was your fault. Minors may receive worker's compensation.

Bibliography

Books and Journals

Adler, Stephen J., *The Jury: Disorder in the Court* (New York: Doubleday, 1994).

Jackson, Sherri, "Too Young to Die: Juveniles and the Death Penalty: A Better Alternative to Killing Our Children: Youth Empowerment," *New England Journal on Criminal and Civil Confinement,* Spring 1996.

Louganis, Greg, *Breaking the Surface* (New York: Random House, 1995).

Paul, Ellen, *The Adoption Directory,* 2d ed. (Detroit: Gale Research, Inc., 1995).

Seminara, George, *Mug Shots: Celebrities Under Arrest* (New York: St. Martins Griffin, 1996).

Streib, Victor L., *Death Penalty for Juveniles* (Bloomington, IN: Indiana University Press, 1987).

White, Ryan, with Ann Marie Cunningham, *Ryan White: My Own Story* (New York: Dial Books, 1991).

Wilson, Jeffrey, and Mary Tomlinson, *Children and the Law,* 2d ed. (Toronto: Butterworth Co., 1986).

Other Resources

Accident Facts 1996, National Safety Council.

America's Fathers and Public Policy, National Research Council, Institute of Medicine, National Academy Press (1994).

American Association for Accreditation of Laboratory Animal Care.

Child Abuse and Neglect: A Look at the States: CWLA Stat Book 1995, Child Welfare League of America.

Child Maltreatment 1994: Reports from the States to the National Center on Child Abuse and Neglect, U.S. Department of Health and Human Services (1996).

Congressional Quarterly Researcher, December, 1995.

Digest of Education Statistics 1996, U.S. Department of Education.

Humane Society of the United States.

Juvenile Offenders and Victims: A National Report, National Center for Juvenile Justice (1995), with *1996 Update on Violence.*

Monthly Labor Review, U.S. Department of Labor.

National Center for State Courts.

The National Law Journal, January 22, 1996.

Occupational Outlook Handbook 1996–1997, U.S. Department of Labor.

The State of America's Children Yearbook 1997, Children's Defense Fund.

Statistical Abstract of the United States 1996, U.S. Department of Commerce.

U.S. Code Congressional and Administrative News, 104th Congress, Vol. 1, pp. 116–117.

Index

About the Author

Photo by Sharon Dennis, Phoenix, Arizona

Thomas A. Jacobs attended Loyola University at Los Angeles and Arizona State University College of Law. He served as an Arizona Assistant Attorney General from 1972 to 1985, handling civil, criminal, and child welfare matters. In 1985, he was appointed to the Maricopa County Superior Court, Juvenile Division, where he presides over delinquency, dependency, severance, and adoption cases. He has published several books and articles on extradition, habeas corpus, children's rights, and other juvenile law topics. A regular speaker and instructor at community functions and educational programs, he also serves as an adjunct professor at the Arizona State University School of Social Work.

Other Great Books from Free Spirit

What Teens Need to Succeed
Proven, Practical Ways to Shape Your Own Future
by Peter L. Benson, Ph.D., Judy Galbraith, M.A., and Pamela Espeland
Based on a national survey, this book describes 40 developmental "assets" all teens need to succeed in life, then gives hundreds of suggestions teens can use to build assets wherever they are. For ages 11 & up.
$14.95; 368 pp.; softcover; illus.; 7¼" x 9¼"

What Do You Stand For?
A Kid's Guide to Building Character
by Barbara A. Lewis
This book empowers children and teens to identify and build character traits. Inspiring quotations, activities, true stories, and resources make this book timely, comprehensive, and fun. For ages 11 & up.
$18.95; 284 pp.; softcover; B&W photos and illus.; 8½" x 11"

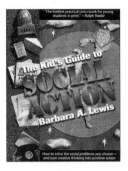

The Kid's Guide to Social Action
How to Solve the Social Problems You Choose— and Turn Creative Thinking into Positive Action
Revised, Expanded, Updated Edition
by Barbara A. Lewis
This exciting, empowering book includes every- thing kids need to make a difference in the world: step-by-step directions for writing letters, doing interviews, raising funds, getting media coverage, and more. For ages 10 & up.
$16.95; 224 pp.; softcover; B&W photos and illus.; 8½" x 11"

To place an order or to request a free catalog of
SELF–HELP FOR KIDS® *and* SELF–HELP FOR TEENS® *materials,*
please write, call, email, or visit our Web site:

Free Spirit Publishing Inc.
400 First Avenue North • Suite 616 • Minneapolis, MN 55401-1724
toll-free 800.735.7323 • local 612.338.2068 • fax 612.337.5050
help4kids@freespirit.com • www.freespirit.com